The Beginner's Guide to the Skies

THE BEGINNER'S GUIDE TO THE
SKIES

A Month-by-Month Handbook
for Stargazers and Planet Watchers

by

Clarence H. Cleminshaw

Thomas Y. Crowell Company
New York Established 1834

Designed by Joy Chu

Manufactured in the United States of America

Library of Congress Cataloging in Publication Data

Cleminshaw, Clarence Higbee, 1902–
The beginner's guide to the skies.
Includes index.
1. Astronomy—Observers' manuals. I. Title.
QB63.C63   523   76-28317
ISBN 0-690-01214-4
2   4   6   8   10   9   7   5   3

Contents

The Beginner's Guide to the Skies

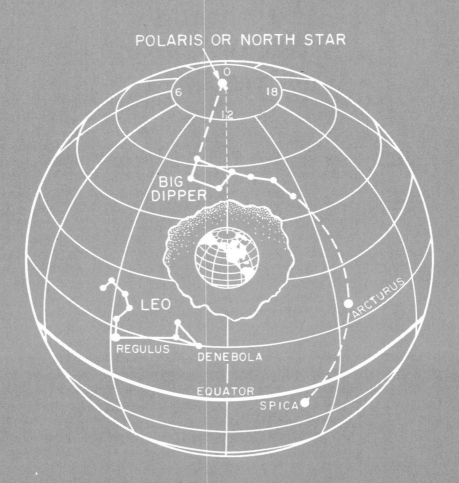

POLARIS OR NORTH STAR

0
6   18
12

BIG
DIPPER

LEO

REGULUS
DENEBOLA

ARCTURUS

EQUATOR
SPICA

Fig. 1-1. The celestial sphere and the earth.

A Start on the Stars

Even in these days of planetaria and increasing popular interest in astronomy, relatively few people are acquainted with the stars. Most people have a good idea of general shapes and positions of the continents on the earth and of the locations of many cities, but their knowledge of the geography of the heavens is usually limited to the Big Dipper. They do not realize how easy it is to make a start on the stars as soon as they have found the Dipper.

When we look at the sky at night, the stars seem to be fastened on the inside of a great bowl or half of a hollow sphere and we appear to be at the center. The other half of this sphere is below our horizon. This complete spherical surface is called the celestial sphere. It is an imaginary construction, of course, and its main use is in describing the apparent positions of the stars, which are their directions as seen from the earth. The real distances of the stars are practically all different, but they are so great that, to all ordinary appearances, they seem to be infinite. The stars appear to be fixed to the celestial sphere.

Fig. 1-1 represents the celestial sphere with a small section of it removed to show the earth at the center. The earth's axis has been extended from the north pole until it intersects the celestial sphere in a point called the north celestial pole. Only one degree away from this pole is Polaris, the Pole Star, which is better known as the North Star. Since in the diagram the northern part of the earth is tilted toward us, the south pole of the earth and the corresponding south celestial pole are not shown. Halfway between the north and south celestial poles is the celestial equator.

Corresponding to the earth's parallels of latitude are the parallels of declination on the celestial sphere. These are drawn at intervals of 15° in the diagram. The declination of a star is its angular distance north or south of the celestial equator. For example, Denebola has a declination of 15° North, and so it appears on the first parallel north of the equator.

Corresponding to the earth's meridians which run from pole to pole are the large circles on the celestial sphere. They are called "hour circles" and there are 24 of them, numbered from 0 to 23. Only half of them are marked in the diagram. In the same way in which we measure longitude along the earth's equator from the Greenwich meridian to any other meridian, we measure what is called right ascension along the celestial equator from the zero hour circle to any other hour circle. The only difference is that right ascension is measured eastward all the way around the celestial equator, whereas longitude is measured halfway around the world to the east and halfway to the west.

In Fig. 1-1 the earth is shown with North America facing toward us. We are looking at the back side of that part of the celestial sphere which includes the Big Dipper. It appears backwards from the way in which it looks to an observer on the earth and similarly all constellations on a celestial globe are reversed. Such a globe represents the celestial sphere as it would appear from the outside. We always see the celestial sphere from the inside.

Under the conditions shown in Fig. 1-1, an observer on the west coast of the United States would see the Big Dipper high in the northern sky, as illustrated in Fig. 1-2. We imagine that we are looking through the transparent dome of the sky from the outside to show what the observer sees when facing north. He is at the center of his circular horizon, which appears foreshortened. The line extending from the south point of the horizon through the zenith (the point directly over his head) and through the north celestial pole (marked approximately by Polaris) is his celestial meridian. It coincides with the hour circle numbered 12.

As the earth rotates eastward (to the right in Fig. 1-1) for two hours, it will bring the observer under the 14th hour circle, which passes near the

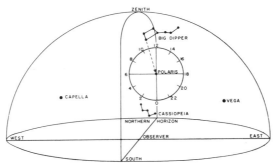

Fig. 1-2. *The northern sky in midevening in the middle of spring. The Big Dipper is above Polaris and Cassiopeia is below it. Vega is low in the northeast and Capella is low in the northwest. The numbers around the circle are the hours of right ascension, which run in a clockwise direction. As the earth rotates to the east, the sky appears to turn to the west and this circle of numbers appears to move counterclockwise. The line passing through the zenith from north to south is the meridian. Number 12 is on that part of the meridian which is above Polaris. Two hours later number 14 would be on the meridian.*

star Arcturus. The Big Dipper will appear to move westward (to the left). In Fig. 1-2 the circle with the numbers marked on it will appear to move in a counterclockwise direction, so that number 14 will be on the celestial meridian directly above Polaris. These numbers refer to the hour circles shown in Fig. 1-1, which are omitted from Fig. 1-2 in order to simplify the diagram.

In both figures a dashed line connects Polaris with the two stars in the bowl of the Big Dipper away from the handle. This line is like the hour hand of a clock, but it moves counterclockwise and takes twice as long to make one rotation.

The rotation of the earth causes all the stars to appear to describe westward circles. The sizes of these circles decrease from the celestial equator to the celestial poles. Since Polaris is only one degree from the north celestial pole, it appears to remain nearly stationary, describing a circle with a radius of only one degree.

An observer at the north pole would always find Polaris one degree from his zenith, and all stars above the horizon would appear to move parallel to the horizon, without rising or setting. If he moves away from the north pole, Polaris will appear to move down toward the horizon and the circle of stars which remain always above the horizon becomes smaller until it finally disappears at the equator.

The radius of this circumpolar circle, as it is called, is always equal to the latitude. This means also that the altitude (angular distance above the horizon) of the celestial pole is equal to the latitude. For example, at the latitude of Minneapolis, 45°N., the north celestial pole is midway between the zenith and the northern horizon, and all stars within 45° of this pole, including the Big Dipper, do not set. However, at the latitude of Houston, 30°N., Polaris is only one-third of the distance up from the horizon to the zenith, and only one of the seven stars of the Big Dipper does not set.

If the earth had only the motion of rotation on its axis, the stars would appear in the same positions with respect to the horizon at the same time each night. In fact, they do occupy the same positions if we measure our time with respect to the stars. If a star appears exactly in the south, it will appear there again after the earth has made a complete rotation of 360°. However, during that interval, which is called a sidereal day, the earth is moving about 1/365 of its way around the sun. Since the earth completes a revolution of 360° around the sun in about 365 days, a line from the earth to the sun sweeps through an angle of about 1° in a day.

In Fig. 1-3 the earth is shown at two positions one day apart. On June 21 the sun appears in the same direction as a certain star. On June 22 the sun appears about 1° east of that star. In order to complete a rotation with respect to the sun, the earth must turn through about 1° more than for a

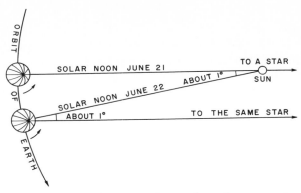

*Fig. 1-3. To complete a rotation with respect to the sun, the earth must turn through about 1°
more than for a rotation with respect to the stars.*

rotation with respect to the stars. It takes the earth about four minutes to turn this extra degree. So the solar day which we use in everday life is about four minutes longer than the true period of the earth's rotation, which is a sidereal day or a day measured with respect to the stars.

If the two stars in the Big Dipper which point to the North Star are directly above it at 10 P.M. on one night, they will reach that position at 9:56 P.M. the next night. They make a complete revolution in 23 hours and 56 minutes of solar time. In other words, the earth makes a complete rotation on its axis in four minutes less than 24 hours. By 10 P.M. these stars will have moved slightly beyond their former position. Thus if one looks at the sky each night at 10 P.M., he will see that the position of the Dipper slowly shifts from night to night in a counterclockwise direction. During 24 hours a line from the Pointers to the pole sweeps through about 361°. At the end of the month the Pointers at 10 P.M. will be 30° beyond their former position at that hour. After six months they will be directly below the pole. After a year of 365 days they will be back at their first position, having completed 366 trips around the pole.

Now we are ready to explain some simple methods for finding the principal stars. The star chart in Fig. 1-4 has four sectors marked on it like pieces of pie. Each one contains most of the brighter stars which are at or near their highest positions in midevening at the middle of each of the four seasons. The circle marked with a continuous line is the celestial equator. The circle marked with a dashed line is the ecliptic, which is the apparent annual path of the sun against the background of the stars. It crosses the equator at the equinoxes. On March 21 the sun reaches the vernal equinox, which is the point from which right ascension is measured. So this point is marked 0 and the other hours are marked along the equator, increasing in a clockwise direction.

4

If the observer were at the north pole, Polaris would always be one degree from overhead. If he were at the equator, his zenith would lie somewhere on the celestial equator, depending on the date and hour. Fig. 1-4 shows his zenith at a latitude of 34°N. in four positions, one for each season. Each one lies on one of the four solid lines radiating from the center of the numbered circle. The length of each radius represents 90°, the angular distance along an hour circle from the equator to the pole. Since 34° is a little more than one-third of 90°, his zenith lies a little more than one-third of the distance from the celestial equator to the north celestial pole.

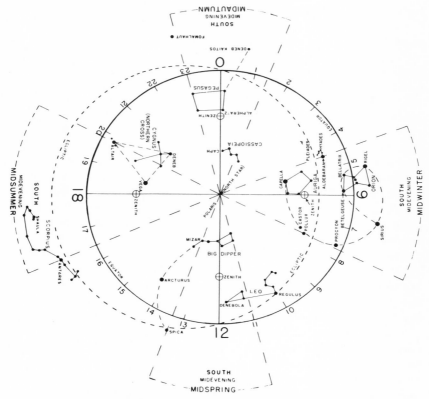

Fig. 1-4. *The four seasonal groups of stars. Of the 20 brightest stars, 15 are marked on this map, the other five being too far south to be shown. The winter sky has seven of these 15 stars, six of which lie along a figure "6", namely, Capella, Pollux, Procyon, Sirius, Rigel, and Betelgeuse. The other one is Aldebaran.*
The summer sky contains Antares and the triangle of Vega, Altair, and Deneb. The spring sky includes Arcturus, Spica, and Regulus, while Fomalhaut is the only first-magnitude star in the autumn sky.

We find the zenith for spring on the radius numbered "12." To look at the Big Dipper, the observer faces north, because that constellation lies between the zenith and the North Star. To see Denebola, which is near number "12" and on the opposite side of the zenith from the Big Dipper, he faces south. He finds Regulus near number "10", which is to the right of number "12," and Arcturus near number "14," which is to the left of number "12." Thus Regulus would be in the southwest and Arcturus in the southeast.

Note that east and west are reversed on star maps from the way they appear on maps of the earth, because the sky and the earth are facing each other. If one looks at the earth from the sky, east is on the right, but if one looks at the sky from the earth, east is on the left. Of course, it is understood that south is at the bottom.

Each of the seven stars in the Big Dipper has a name, but only the name of the most interesting star will be mentioned here. It is Mizar and is the middle one of the three stars forming the handle. As an aid to memory, it should be noted that the first two letters of "Mizar" and of "middle" are the same. Mizar was the first double star to be discovered with the telescope, its two stars were the first components of a double star to be photographed, and one of its components was the first spectroscopic binary to be discovered. Later the other component was also found by means of the spectroscope to consist of two stars. Too close to Mizar to be shown on the chart, but easily visible to the unaided eye is a fainter star named Alcor, which is also a spectroscopic binary. Thus there are six stars at the middle of the handle of the Big Dipper, where only two can be seen with the naked eye and only one may be noticed with a hasty glance.

Imagine a curve passing through the handle and prolonged about as far as the total length of the Dipper. There it will meet Arcturus. Thus we have followed an arc to find Arcturus, and that may help in remembering that name. If this arc is continued about an equal distance, as indicated by the dashed line on the map, it will come to Spica. It is interesting to notice that Mizar and Spica have the same right ascension of $13^h 22^m$. For that reason a straight dashed line has been drawn from the pole through these stars to form one side of this sector.

The sides of the sectors were not drawn to include necessarily within each sector all the important stars of that season. They were drawn so as to pass through two stars having about the same right ascension or through two stars whose right ascension differs by about 12 hours. When the line through Spica and Mizar is extended on the other side of the pole, it passes through a star in Cassiopeia named Ruchbah, whose right ascension is $1^h 22^m$, just 12 hours less.

In the same way a line passes through the two Pointers in the bowl of the Dipper, whose numbers are $10^h 59^m$ and $11^h 01^m$, and also through the two western stars of Pegasus, whose numbers are 23^h 01^m and 23^h 02^m. Similarly the sides of the summer and winter sectors pass through pairs of stars whose numbers differ by about 12 hours. The positions of Altair and Pollux are 19^h 48^m and 7^h 42^m, while those of Antares and Aldebaran are 16^h 26^m and 4^h 33^m. The last two stars lie close to the ecliptic, as do Regulus and Spica. It will be noticed that these four stars all lie along one half of the ecliptic. There are no first-magnitude stars very near the other half of the ecliptic.

Coming back to the spring stars, we can see that an easy way to find the constellation of Leo is to draw a line southward from the Pointers of the Big Dipper. That line will pass through the middle of Leo, which consists of a small right triangle and a sickle. The star at the left corner of this triangle is Denebola. In the old mythological figure of the Lion, it marked the Lion's tail. That is the origin of the name, "deneb" meaning "tail" in Arabic. The sickle opens to the west and has Regulus at the bottom of its handle. For those who like aids to memory, we can call 12 a dozen and note that the Dozen line passes through the Dipper and near Denebola, giving us three words beginning with D.

Moving on to the summer sky, which has the 18-hour circle passing through the middle of it, we find the very bright star Vega near the zenith. A large triangle is formed by Vega, Deneb, and Altair. Deneb marks the tail of Cygnus, the Swan, which is better known as the Northern Cross. Altair can be identified by its two little guard stars pointing in a line to Vega.

Antares also has a fainter star on either side of it and they are spaced about the way the two are near Altair, but the line through them and Antares is slightly curved. Antares lies nearly on a straight line extended from the upright part of the Northern Cross. This does not appear to be so on the star chart, because of the distortion produced on a flat map. On this map the distortion is worst on the outside, so that the constellation of Scorpius is spread out too much in an east-west direction. In the sky, Scorpius really looks like a scorpion, with its tail curving up over its back. There are two stars close together at the end of the tail. The brighter one is Shaula.

The central line of the autumn sky is marked with a zero. If we call it an aught, it sounds like the first syllable of autumn, and that may help us to associate the two words. The principal constellation of autumn is Pegasus, which is most easily recognized as a square. However, we could imagine an oval drawn through the four corners of the square and that would remind us that the zero line passes through Pegasus. Lines through the eastern and western sides of the square point to the North Star, the western side lying nearly on the 23-hour circle and the eastern side lying close to the zero line. The northeast corner of the square is marked by Alpheratz, which passes very close to the zenith. Lying very nearly on the zero line and halfway from Alpheratz to the North Star is Caph. This is a good way to find the North Star in the autumn, when the Big Dipper is very near the horizon or even partly below it. Just draw a line from Alpheratz to Caph and extend it an equal distance to the North Star. Caph is at the western end of Cassiopeia, which resembles a W.

Two more stars can be found by drawing lines to the south from the sides of the Square of Pegasus. Fomalhaut lies very close to the 23-hour circle and Deneb Kaitos is between the zero- and 1-hour circles.

The winter sky has about twice as many bright stars in it as the sky of any other season. It is centered on the 6-hour line. The map shows that a large figure 6 can be drawn through eight bright stars. A little northwest of the zenith is Capella, the cap or top of the figure. The next star is Castor, which also begins with a C. The following two stars, Pollux and Procyon, begin with a P. The loop at the bottom of the 6 is formed by Sirius, Rigel, Bellatrix, and Betelgeuse, the last two names beginning with a B.

The finest constellation in the whole sky is Orion, whose seven principal stars are among the 67 brightest stars. Orion's belt contains three stars in nearly a straight line about 3° long. The ends of the belt can be joined to the other four stars to form a figure which looks like a butterfly. A line drawn through Orion's belt to the southeast passes through Sirius, the brightest appearing star in the sky.

As a further aid to remembering its approximate location, we might notice that Capella lies near the 5-hour line and is part of a 5-sided figure, Auriga. Also we find a little to the southwest a V, which stands for 5, formed by Aldebaran and the cluster of stars called the Hyades. This V marks the head of Taurus, the Bull, in the shoulders of which is another star cluster, the Pleiades.

And so we have gone around the chart, which shows the outlines of eight constellations, two for each season, and the positions of two dozen stars. These can be summarized as follows:

Autumn (0-Hour Circle)

Constellations	Stars	
Cassiopeia	Alpheratz	Deneb Kaitos
Pegasus	Caph	Fomalhaut

Seasonal Groups of Stars

Winter (6-Hour Circle)

Constellations
Auriga
Orion

Stars

Aldebaran	Pollux
Bellatrix	Procyon
Betelgeuse	Rigel
Capella	Sirius
Castor	

Spring (12-Hour Circle)

Constellations
Big Dipper
Leo

Stars

Arcturus	Regulus
Denebola	Spica
Mizar	

Summer (18-Hour Circle)

Constellations
Northern Cross
Scorpius

Stars

Altair	Shaula
Antares	Vega
Deneb	

Exploring the Sky
from the Big Dipper

The accompanying diagram shows that if the line from the two Pointer stars of the Big Dipper to Polaris is continued far enough it runs into one side of the Square of Pegasus. Also a line from the star joining the handle to the bowl of the Dipper can be drawn through Polaris, one end of the "W" of Cassiopeia and another side of the Square.

The seven stars in the Dipper are designated by Greek letters according to position. Alpha and Beta are the two Pointers to Polaris. The other two stars in the bowl are Gamma and Delta. A line through them leads to Vega in one direction and to Regulus in the other. Lines connecting Vega, Deneb and Altair form what is known as the "Summer Triangle." This is not a constellation but a convenient aid to learning these stars. Vega belongs to Lyra, Deneb to Cygnus and Altair to Aquila.

Fig. 2-1.

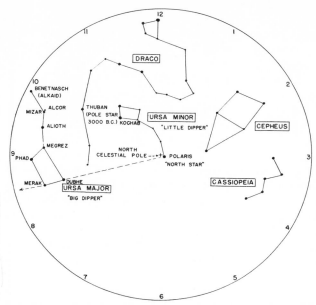

Fig. 2-2. How to tell time by the stars. The hour hand is a line from Polaris through the Pointers of the Big Dipper, and is in the position of 8½. The date is July 15, which is 6½ months past January 1. The sum of these numbers is 15. Double that and subtract from 40¼. The result is 10¼, and the time is about 10:15 P.M. Add one hour for daylight saving time.

Regulus is the brightest star in Leo, consisting of a sickle and a triangle. The second brightest star in Leo is Denebola.

A line from Delta to Alpha leads to the constellation of Auriga, a pentagon. Its brightest star is Capella. A line from Delta to Beta leads to Pollux, the brighter of the Twins. The other one is Castor.

The dashed line extending from the handle of the Dipper shows how to find Arcturus and Spica. Just follow the arc to Arcturus and spiral to Spica.

In the evening, the Dipper is below the pole in autumn, to the right in winter, above the pole in spring, and to the left in summer. Thus we have a great clock in the sky which tells the seasons and the hours of the night. With a little practice, one can estimate the time quite well. Let us see how we can arrive at a rule which will make this easy to remember.

Imagine the dial of a clock in the sky with the North Star in the center. The 12 on the dial should be directly above the North Star and nearly overhead. The 6 will be directly below the North Star and about on the horizon. The 3 will be to the east and the 9 to the west of the North Star, both lying on a horizontal line through the North Star. The Pointers of the Big Dipper serve as the hour hand. The indicated time can easily be read to the nearest quarter hour. Add to this the number of months which have elapsed since January 1, to the nearest quarter month. Double this sum and subtract the result from 16¼, or from 40¼, if the result is greater than 16¼. The answer is the time in hours P.M. If the answer is greater than 12, subtract 12 and get the time in hours A.M.

An example will make this clear. The Pointers are in the position of 8½. The date is July 15, which is 6½ months past January 1. The sum of these two numbers is 15. Twice that is 30. Subtract 30 from 40¼, and the answer is 10¼. The time is about 10:15 P.M.

This method gives the local time to the nearest quarter hour. To change to standard time, a small correction must be added for a place west of the standard meridian and subtracted for a place to the east. Los Angeles has a longitude of 7 hours and 53 minutes, and so it is 7 minutes east of the standard meridian. If it was the place of observation in the above example, then the Pacific Standard Time would be about 10:08.

The Monthly Star Maps

There are two star maps for each month. Those on the left-hand pages show the principal stars and constellations in the evening sky at about 9 P.M. Standard Time at the middle of each month. They are made for the latitude of 34° North, but they can be used anywhere in the continental United States (and at similar latitudes all over the world) throughout the month, showing the sky at 10 P.M. on the first and at 8 P.M. on the last of the month.

The maps on the right-hand pages show the sky at about 5 A.M. at the middle of each month except May, June, July and August, when the sky is shown at about 3 A.M.

To use a map, hold it vertically and turn it so that the point of the compass toward which you are facing shows on the bottom of the map.

The locations of four planets are given for every month for the years from 1977 through 1988. Mercury is not included here, because it moves too rapidly and appears too near the sun most of the time. See page 68 for the times when it can be observed.

Venus, the brightest planet, is brighter than any of the stars and it never appears more than about 45° from the sun. Therefore, when it is in the evening sky it is near the western horizon, and when it is in the early morning sky it is near the eastern horizon. Its location is indicated at the bottom of each of the twenty-four maps. If any year from 1977 to 1988 is missing from both the evening and predawn maps of any month, that means that Venus appears too near the sun to be easily visible at that time.

The twelve constellations of the zodiac in which Mars, Jupiter and Saturn appear are given for each month from 1977 to 1988. Six of them are listed below the evening star map and the other six below the predawn map. They are arranged in order from the western horizon to the eastern horizon, because that is the direction in which the planets move from month to month.

Since the predawn map is only eight hours later than the evening map, several constellations of the zodiac appear on both maps. For example, on the January maps, Gemini, Cancer and Leo are in the east in the evening sky and in the west in the predawn sky. An asterisk after the name of a constellation indicates that the sun is in that region for at least a part of that month, and hence the planets there would not be visible.

The figures show the years, with the first two figures (19) omitted, when Mars, Jupiter and Saturn appear in each constellation. Using January again as an example, we find that Mars is in Cancer in 1978, Leo in 1980, Virgo in 1982 and 1984, Libra in 1986, and Scorpius in 1988. In the odd years, Mars in January is in Sagittarius in 1977 and 1979, Capricornus in 1981, Aquarius in 1983 and 1985, and Pisces in 1987. Thus we see that Mars during an average interval of two years moves all the way around the zodiac and into the next constellation to the east. Sometimes it skips one constellation and at other times it comes back to the same constellation two years later. This is because its speed varies and because the constellations of the zodiac range in length from about 20° for Cancer to about 45° for Virgo.

Since Jupiter revolves around the sun in about twelve years, it spends about one year in each constellation. Since Saturn's period is nearly thirty years, it is in each constellation for an average of nearly two and one-half years.

When using a star map to identify the stars, illuminate it with a red light. This will enable you to see fainter stars more quickly than if you use white light.

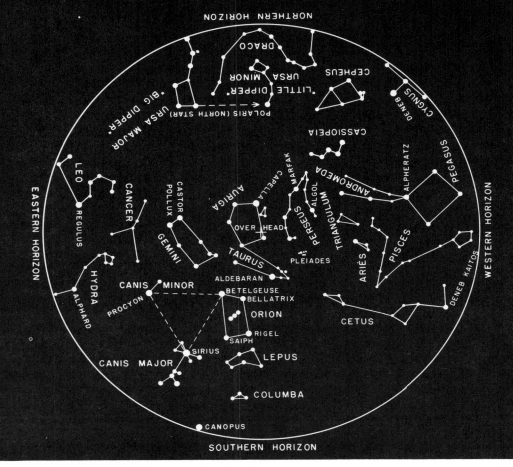

Fig. 2-3.

THE EVENING SKY IN JANUARY

Locations of Planets (1977–88)

	Aquarius	Pisces	Aries	Taurus	Gemini	Cancer
Mars	83, 85	87				78
Jupiter		87–88	77	78		79
Saturn						77

Venus in early evening sky near western horizon in 1977, 1980, 1983, 1985, 1988.

This map shows the stars at mid-month at these Standard Times:

September	5 A.M.	December	11 P.M.
October	3 A.M.	January	9 P.M.
November	1 A.M.	February	7 P.M.

14

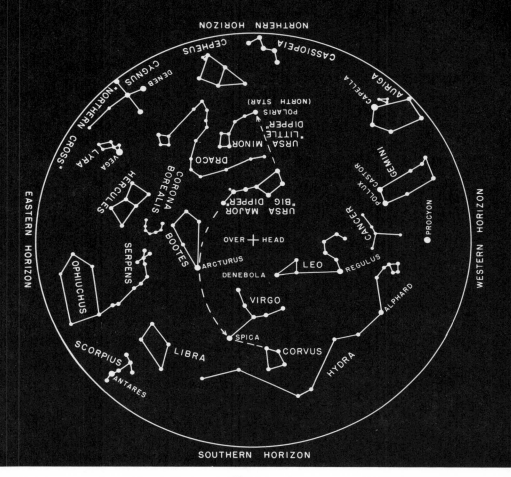

Fig. 2-4.

THE PREDAWN SKY IN JANUARY

Locations of Planets (1977–88)

	Leo	Virgo	Libra	Scorpius	Sagittarius *	Capricornus *
Mars	80	82, 84	86	88	77, 79	81
Jupiter	80	81	82	83	84–85	86
Saturn	78–79	80–83	84–85	86–87	88	

* Sun in constellation.

Venus in early morning sky near eastern horizon in 1979, 1981, 1984, 1987.

This map shows the stars at mid-month at these Standard Times:

January	5 A.M.	March	1 A.M.
February	3 A.M.	April	11 P.M.
		May	9 P.M.

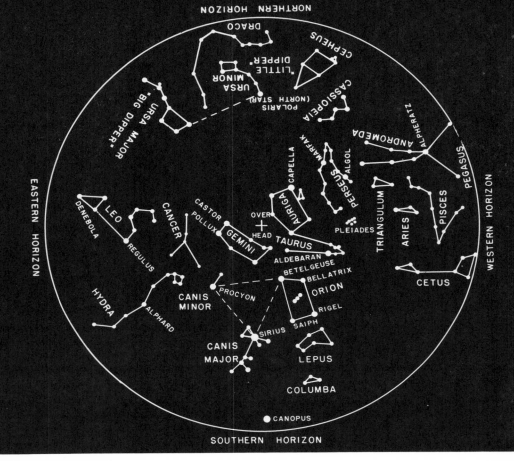

Fig. 2-5.

THE EVENING SKY IN FEBRUARY

Locations of Planets (1977–88)

	Pisces	Aries	Taurus	Gemini	Cancer	Leo
Mars	83, 85	87		78		80
Jupiter	87–88	77	78		79	80
Saturn					77	78–79

Venus in early evening sky near western horizon in 1977, 1980, 1983, 1985, 1988.

This map shows the stars at mid-month at these Standard Times:

October	5 A.M.	January	11 P.M.
November	3 A.M.	February	9 P.M.
December	1 A.M.	March	7 P.M.

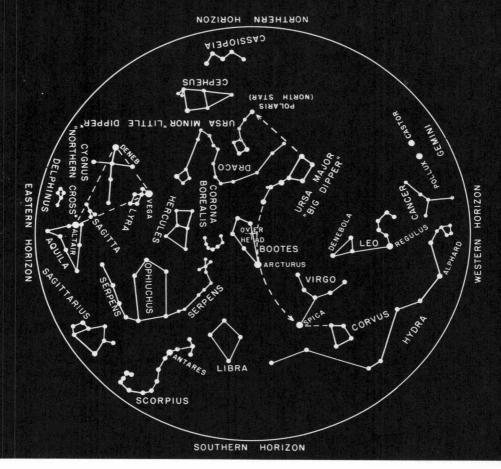

Fig. 2-6.

THE PREDAWN SKY IN FEBRUARY

Locations of Planets (1977–88)

	Virgo	Libra	Scorpius	Sagittarius	Capricornus *	Aquarius *
Mars	82	84	86, 88		77, 79	81
Jupiter	81	82	83	84	85	86
Saturn	80–83	84–85	86–87	88		

* Sun in constellation.

Venus in early morning sky near eastern horizon in 1979, 1981, 1984, 1987.

This map shows the stars at mid-month at these Standard Times:

February	5 A.M.	April	1 A.M.
March	3 A.M.	May	11 P.M.
		June	9 P.M.

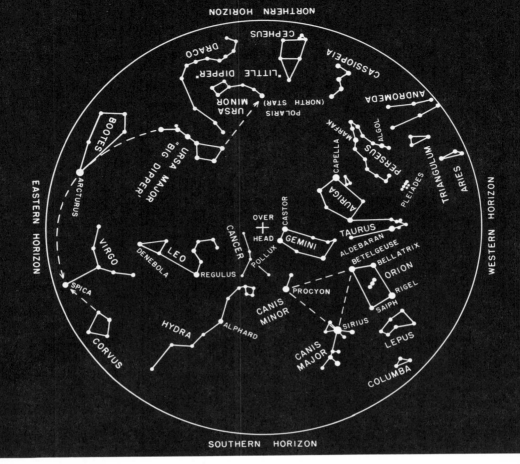

Fig. 2-7.

THE EVENING SKY IN MARCH

Locations of Planets (1977–88)

	Aries	Taurus	Gemini	Cancer	Leo	Virgo
Mars	85, 87		78		80	82
Jupiter	88	77–78		79	80	81–82
Saturn				77	78–79	80–83

Venus in early evening sky near western horizon in 1977, 1978, 1980, 1983, 1985, 1986, 1988.

This map shows the stars at mid-month at these Standard Times:

November	5 A.M.	February	11 P.M.
December	3 A.M.	March	9 P.M.
January	1 A.M.	April	7 P.M.

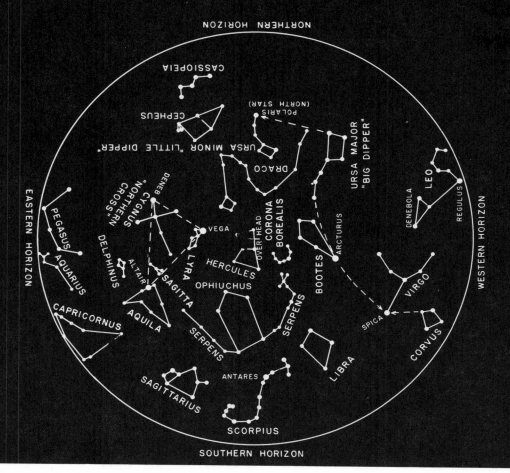

Fig. 2-8.

THE PREDAWN SKY IN MARCH

Locations of Planets (1977–88)

	Libra	*Scorpius*	*Sagittarius*	*Capricornus*	*Aquarius* *	*Pisces* *
Mars	84	86	88	77	79	81, 83
Jupiter		83	84	85	86	87
Saturn	84–85	86–87	88			

* Sun in constellation.

Venus in early morning sky near eastern horizon in 1979, 1982, 1984, 1987.

This map shows the stars at mid-month at these Standard Times:

March	5 A.M.	May	1 A.M.
April	3 A.M.	June	11 P.M.
		July	9 P.M.

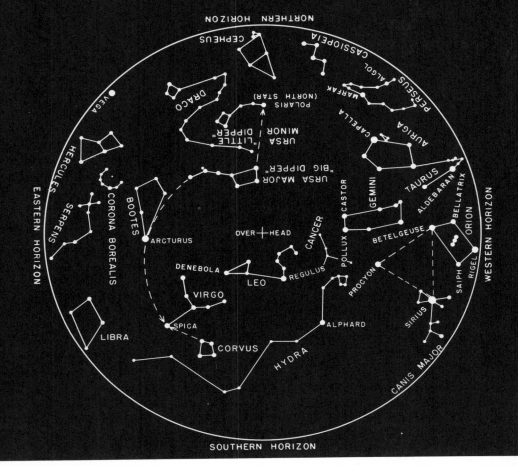

Fig. 2-9.

THE EVENING SKY IN APRIL

Locations of Planets (1977–88)

	Taurus	Gemini	Cancer	Leo	Virgo	Libra
Mars	87		78	80	82	84
Jupiter	77	78	79	80	81–82	
Saturn			77	78–79	80–83	84–85

Venus in early evening sky near western horizon in 1978, 1980, 1983, 1986, 1988.

This map shows the stars at mid-month at these Standard Times:

December	5 A.M.	February	1 A.M.
January	3 A.M.	March	11 P.M.
		April	9 P.M.

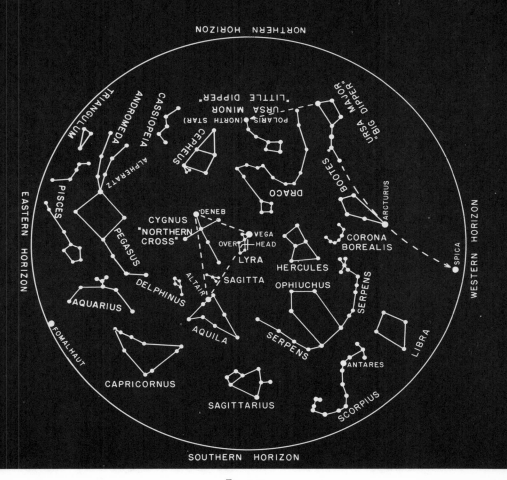

Fig. 2-10.

THE PREDAWN SKY IN APRIL

Locations of Planets (1977–88)

	Scorpius	Sagittarius	Capricornus	Aquarius	Pisces *	Aries *
Mars		86	88	77	79, 81	83, 85
Jupiter	83	84	85	86	87	88
Saturn	86, 87	88				

* Sun in constellation.

Venus in early morning sky near eastern horizon in 1979, 1982, 1984, 1987.

This map shows the stars at mid-month at these Standard Times:

April	5 A.M.	July	11 P.M.
May	3 A.M.	August	9 P.M.
June	1 A.M.	September	7 P.M.

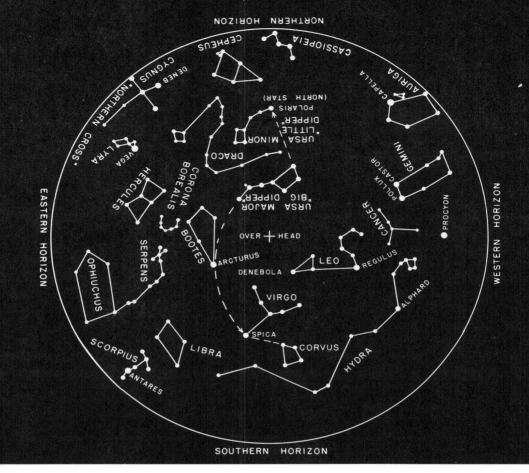

Fig. 2-11.

THE EVENING SKY IN MAY

Locations of Planets (1977–88)

	Gemini	Cancer	Leo	Virgo	Libra	Scorpius
Mars		78	80	82	84	
Jupiter	78	79	80	81, 82		83
Saturn		77	78–79	80–83	84–85	86–87

Venus in early evening sky near western horizon in 1978, 1980, 1983, 1986, 1988.

This map shows the stars at mid-month at these Standard Times:

January	5 A.M.	March	1 A.M.
February	3 A.M.	April	11 P.M.
	May	9 P.M.	

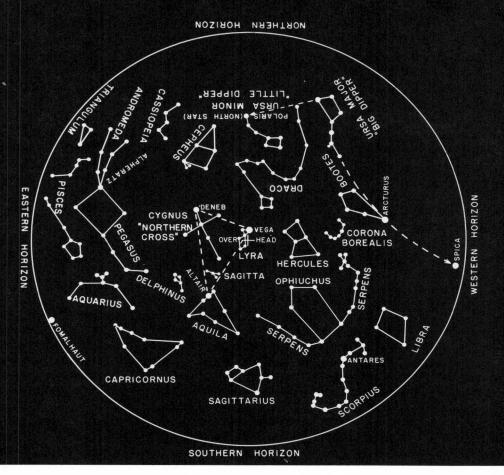

Fig. 2-12.

THE PREDAWN SKY IN MAY

Locations of Planets (1977–88)

	Sagittarius	Capricornus	Aquarius	Pisces	Aries *	Taurus *
Mars	86	88		77	79, 81	83, 85, 87
Jupiter	84	85	86	87	88	77
Saturn	88					

* Sun in constellation.

Venus in early morning sky near eastern horizon in 1977, 1979, 1982, 1985, 1987.

This map shows the stars at mid-month at these Standard Times:

May	3 A.M.	July	11 P.M.
June	1 A.M.	August	9 P.M.
September	7 P.M.		

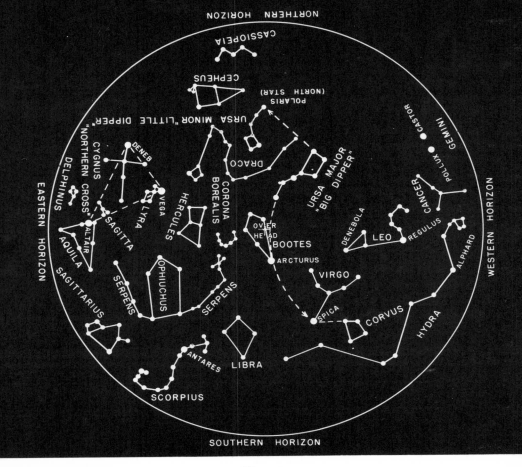

Fig. 2-13.

THE EVENING SKY IN JUNE

Locations of Planets (1977–88)

	Cancer	Leo	Virgo	Libra	Scorpius	Sagittarius
Mars		78, 80	82	84		86
Jupiter	79	80	81–82		83	84
Saturn	77	78–79	80–83	84–85	86–87	88

Venus in early evening sky near western horizon in 1978, 1981, 1983, 1986.

This map shows the stars at mid-month at these Standard Times:

February	5 A.M.	April	1 A.M.
March	3 A.M.	May	11 P.M.
		June	9 P.M.

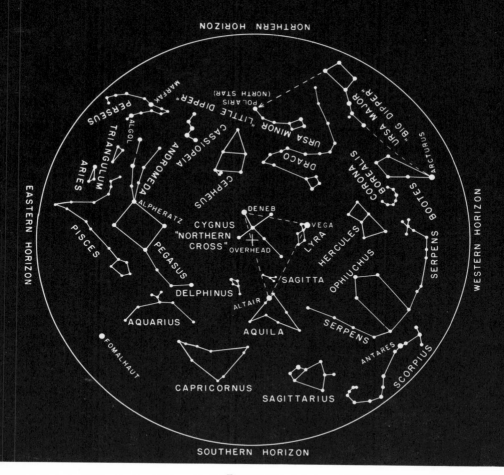

Fig. 2-14.

THE PREDAWN SKY IN JUNE

Locations of Planets (1977–88)

	Capricornus	Aquarius	Pisces	Aries	Taurus *	Gemini *
Mars		88		77	79, 81, 83	85, 87
Jupiter	85		86–87	88	77	78
Saturn						

* Sun in constellation.

Venus in early morning sky near eastern horizon in 1977, 1979, 1982, 1985, 1987.

This map shows the stars at mid-month at these Standard Times:

June	3 A.M.	August	11 P.M.
July	1 A.M.	September	9 P.M.
	October	7 P.M.	

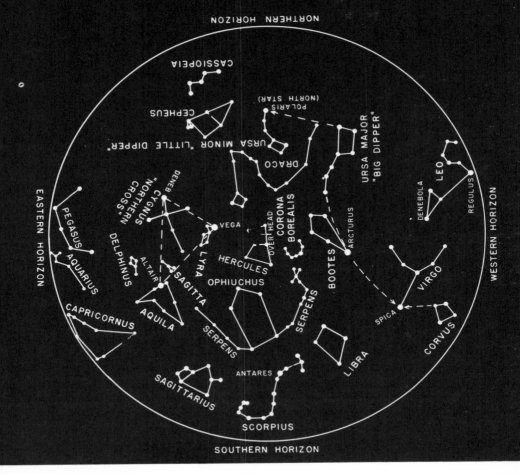

Fig. 2-15.

THE EVENING SKY IN JULY

Locations of Planets (1977–88)

	Leo	Virgo	Libra	Scorpius	Sagittarius	Capricornus
Mars	78	80, 82	84		86	
Jupiter	80	81–82		83	84	85
Saturn	77–79	80–83	84–85	86–87	88	

Venus in early evening sky near western horizon in 1978, 1981, 1983, 1986.

This map shows the stars at mid-month at these Standard Times:

March	5 A.M.	May	1 A.M.
April	3 A.M.	June	11 P.M.
		July	9 P.M.

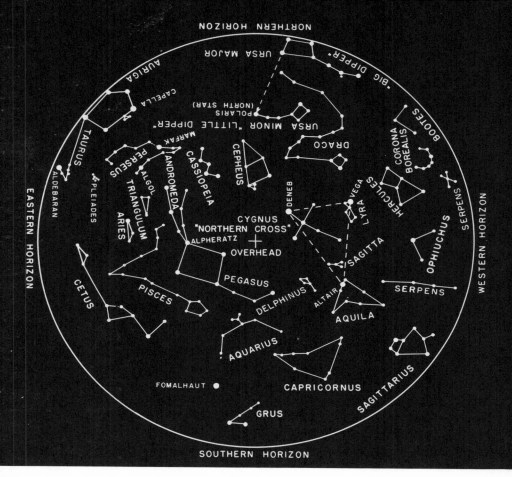

Fig. 2-16.

THE PREDAWN SKY IN JULY

Locations of Planets (1977–88)

	Aquarius	Pisces	Aries	Taurus	Gemini *	Cancer *
Mars	88			77, 79	81, 83	85, 87
Jupiter		86–87		77, 88	78	79
Saturn						

* Sun in constellation.

Venus in early morning sky near eastern horizon in 1977, 1980, 1982,
1985, 1988.

This map shows the stars at mid-month at these Standard Times:

July	3 A.M.	September	11 P.M.
August	1 A.M.	October	9 P.M.
	November	7 P.M.	

27

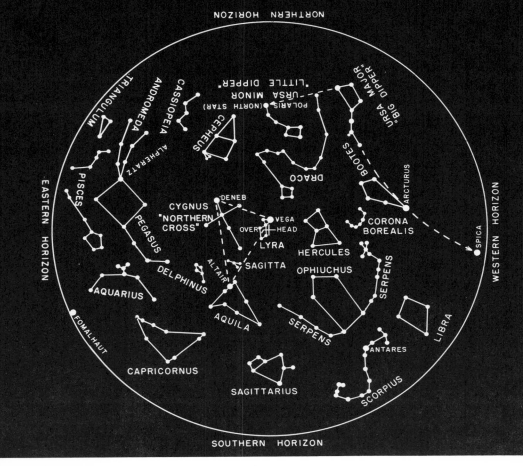

Fig. 2-17.

THE EVENING SKY IN AUGUST

Locations of Planets (1977–88)

	Virgo	Libra	Scorpius	Sagittarius	Capricornus	Aquarius
Mars	78, 80	82, 84		86		
Jupiter	81–82		83	84	85	86
Saturn	80–83	84–85	86–87	88		

Venus in early evening sky near western horizon in 1978, 1981, 1984, 1986.

This map shows the stars at mid-month at these Standard Times:

April	5 A.M.	July	11 P.M.
May	3 A.M.	August	9 P.M.
June	1 A.M.	September	7 P.M.

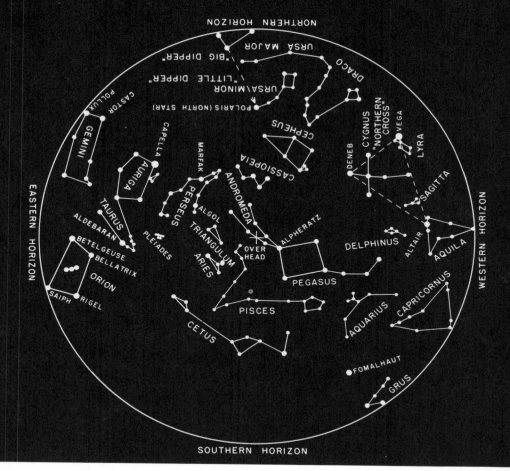

Fig. 2-18.

THE PREDAWN SKY IN AUGUST

Locations of Planets (1977–88)

	Pisces	Aries	Taurus	Gemini	Cancer *	Leo *
Mars	88		77	79, 81	83, 85	87
Jupiter		87	88	77–78		79–80
Saturn						77–79

* Sun in constellation.

Venus in early morning sky near eastern horizon in 1977, 1980, 1982, 1985, 1988.

This map shows the stars at mid-month at these Standard Times:

August	3 A.M.	October	11 P.M.
September	1 A.M.	November	9 P.M.
	December	7 P.M.	

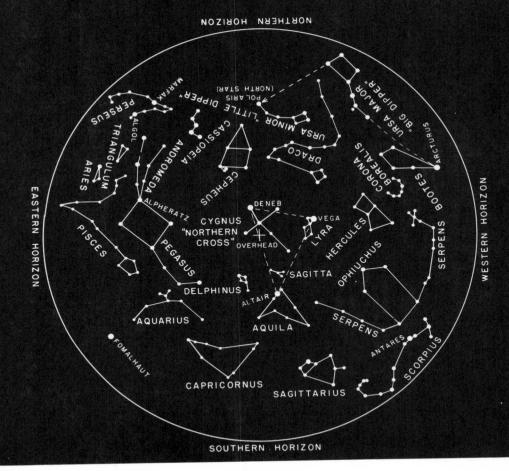

Fig. 2-19.

THE EVENING SKY IN SEPTEMBER

Locations of Planets (1977–88)

	Libra	Scorpius	Sagittarius	Capricornus	Aquarius	Pisces
Mars	80, 82	84		86		88
Jupiter	82	83	84	85	86	
Saturn	84–85	86–87	88			

*Venus in early evening sky near western horizon in 1978, 1981,
1984, 1986.*

This map shows the stars at mid-month at these Standard Times:

June	3 A.M.	August	11 P.M.
July	1 A.M.	September	9 P.M.
		October	7 P.M.

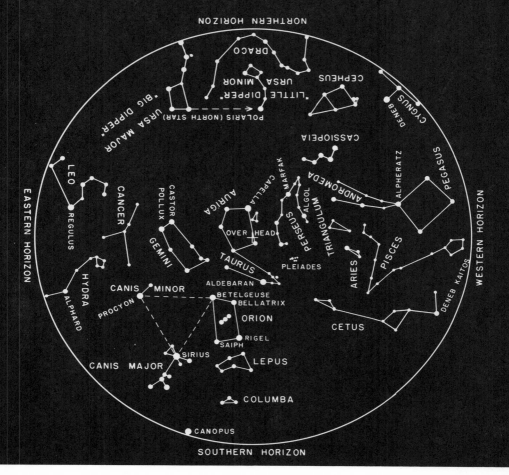

Fig. 2-20.

THE PREDAWN SKY IN SEPTEMBER

Locations of Planets (1977–88)

	Aries	Taurus	Gemini	Cancer	Leo *	Virgo *
Mars			77, 79	81	83, 85, 87	78
Jupiter	87	88	77	78	79–80	81
Saturn					77–79	80–83

* Sun in constellation.

Venus in early morning sky near eastern horizon in 1977, 1980, 1982, 1985, 1988.

This map shows the stars at mid-month at these Standard Times:

September	5 A.M.	December	11 P.M.
October	3 A.M.	January	9 P.M.
November	1 A.M.	February	7 P.M.

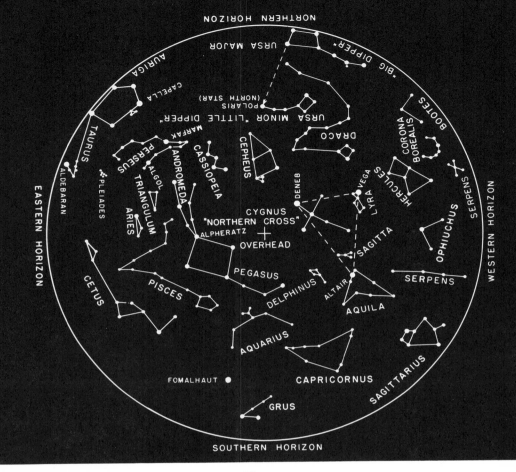

Fig. 2-21.

THE EVENING SKY IN OCTOBER

Locations of Planets (1977–88)

	Libra	Scorpius	Sagittarius	Capricornus	Aquarius	Pisces
Mars	78	80, 82	84	86		88
Jupiter	82	83	84	85	86	87
Saturn	84–85	86–87	88			

Venus in early evening sky near western horizon in 1978, 1979, 1981, 1984, 1986, 1987.

This map shows the stars at mid-month at these Standard Times:

July	3 A.M.	September	11 P.M.
August	1 A.M.	October	9 P.M.
	November	7 P.M.	

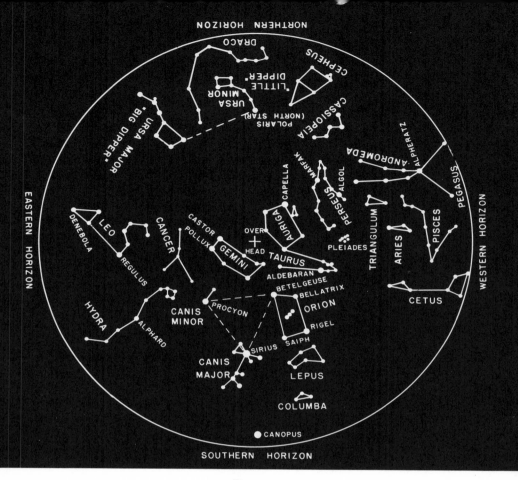

Fig. 2-22.

THE PREDAWN SKY IN OCTOBER

Locations of Planets (1977–88)

	Aries	Taurus	Gemini	Cancer	Leo	Virgo *
Mars			77	79	81, 83, 85	87
Jupiter		88	77	78	79	80–81
Saturn					77–79	80–83

* Sun in constellation.

Venus in early morning sky near eastern horizon in 1977, 1980, 1983, 1985, 1988.

This map shows the stars at mid-month at these Standard Times:

October	5 A.M.	January	11 P.M.
November	3 A.M.	February	9 P.M.
December	1 A.M.	March	7 P.M.

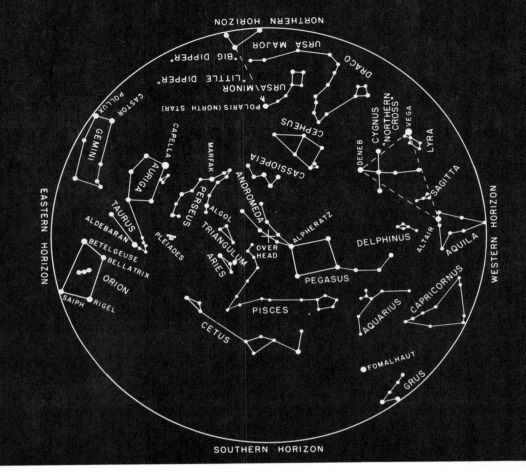

Fig. 2-23.

THE EVENING SKY IN NOVEMBER

Locations of Planets (1977–88)

	Sagittarius	Capricornus	Aquarius	Pisces	Aries	Taurus
Mars	82, 84	86		88		
Jupiter	84	85	86	87		88
Saturn	88					

Venus in early evening sky near western horizon in 1979, 1981, 1984, 1987.

This map shows the stars at mid-month at these Standard Times:

August	3 A.M.	October	11 P.M.
September	1 A.M.	November	9 P.M.
		December	7 P.M.

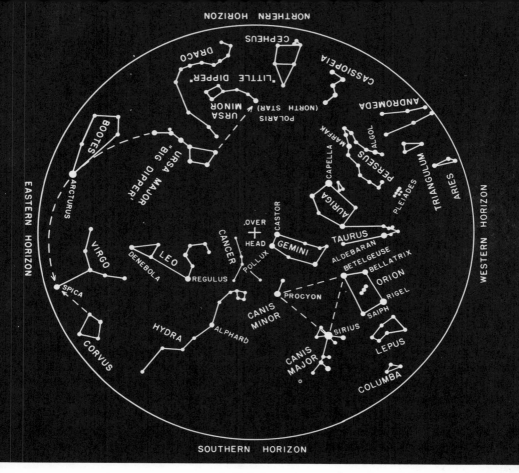

Fig. 2-24.

THE PREDAWN SKY IN NOVEMBER

Locations of planets (1977–88)

	Gemini	Cancer	Leo	Virgo	Libra *	Scorpius *
Mars		77	79, 81	83, 85, 87		78, 80
Jupiter	77	78	79	80–81	82	83
Saturn			77–78	79–82	83–84	85–87

* Sun in constellation.

Venus in early morning sky near eastern horizon in 1977, 1980, 1983, 1985, 1988.

This map shows the stars at mid-month at these Standard Times:

November	5 A.M.	February	11 P.M.
December	3 A.M.	March	9 P.M.
January	1 A.M.	April	7 P.M.

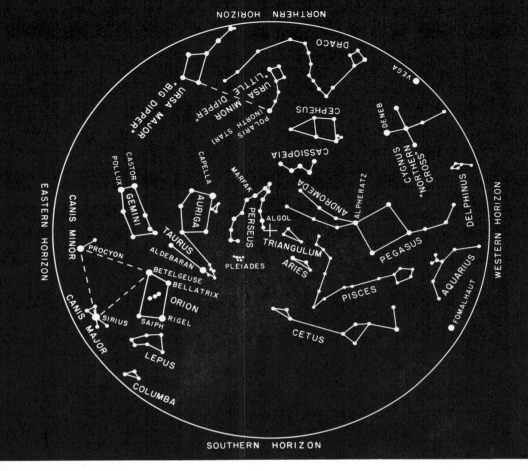

Fig. 2-25.

THE EVENING SKY IN DECEMBER

Locations of Planets (1977–88)

	Capricornus	Aquarius	Pisces	Aries	Taurus	Gemini
Mars	82, 84	86	88			
Jupiter	85	86	87		88	77
Saturn						

Venus in early evening sky near western horizon in 1979, 1981, 1984, 1987.

This map shows the stars at mid-month at these Standard Times:

September	3 A.M.	November	11 P.M.
October	1 A.M.	December	9 P.M.
		January	7 P.M.

36

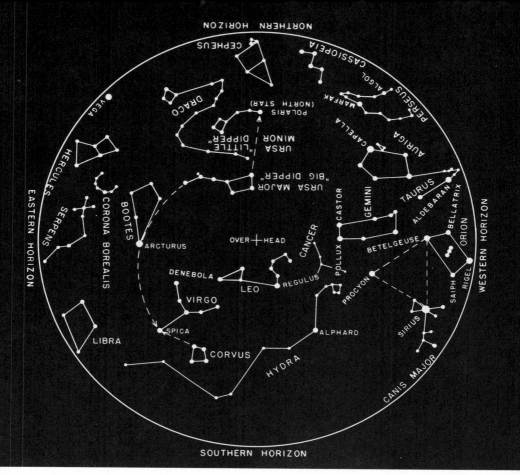

Fig. 2-26.

THE PREDAWN SKY IN DECEMBER

Locations of Planets (1977–88)

	Cancer	Leo	Virgo	Libra	Scorpius *	Sagittarius *
Mars	77	79	81, 83, 85	87		78, 80
Jupiter	78	79	80–81	82	83	84
Saturn		77–78	79–82	83–84	85–87	88

* Sun in constellation.

Venus in early morning sky near eastern horizon in 1978, 1980, 1983,.
1986, 1988.

This map shows the stars at mid-month at these Standard Times:

December	5 A.M.	February	1 A.M.
January	3 A.M.	March	11 P.M.
	April	9 P.M.	

The
Star
Chart

The star chart on pages 40–41 shows the principal stars and constellations from the north celestial pole at the center to 60° south of the celestial equator. The numbers from 0 through 23 along the equator (solid circle) mark the hours of right ascension. Declination is indicated at intervals of 30° along the four dashed hour lines, 0, 6, 12 and 18, which are drawn from the center to the edge of the chart. The other dashed hour lines are shown only south of the equator, in order to avoid crowding around the center.

The curved dashed line crossing the equator at 0 and 12 is the ecliptic, which is the apparent annual path of the sun among the stars. It is inclined 23½° to the equator, so that it crosses the 6-hour line at a declination of 23½° North and the 18-hour line at a declination of 23½° South. The apparent annual motion of the sun is to the east, which is clockwise on the chart. Its position can be roughly determined for any date by noting that its right ascension is 0 hours on March 21 (vernal equinox), 6 hours on June 21 (summer solstice), 12 hours on September 23 (autumnal equinox) and 18 hours on December 22 (winter solstice).

The ecliptic is the central line of the zodiac, which is an imaginary belt of twelve constellations containing the paths of the moon and planets.

The constellations appear on the chart in capital letters and are listed alphabetically in the accompanying table. The approximate right ascension (R.A.) in hours and declination (Dec.) in degrees are given for each constellation. Plus means north and minus means south.

The stars are designated by small letters of the Greek alphabet. Usually the brightest star of each constellation is called Alpha, the second brightest Beta, and so on. In some cases this arrangement is not followed. For example, the seven stars in the Big Dipper are lettered according to position, beginning at the front of the bowl and out along the handle.

The special names of sixty-five stars appear on the chart in small letters and in the accompanying alphabetical list. Each name is followed by its Greek letter and the genitive case of the constellation to which it belongs. Right ascension is usually given in hours and minutes, but for our purpose of finding the star on the chart it is sufficient to give its position to the nearest tenth of an hour of right ascension and to the nearest degree of declination.

The last column lists the star's magnitude, which is a measure of its brightness. About 2,000 years ago twenty of the brightest stars were assigned to the first magnitude. Those a little fainter, like the North Star, were called second magnitude, and so on to the faintest stars visible to the naked eye, which were called sixth magnitude.

It was found that an average star of the first magnitude is about 100 times as bright as one of the sixth magnitude. This difference of five magnitudes was fixed to correspond to a difference of 100 times in brightness.

The light-ratio from one magnitude to the next is the fifth root of 100, which is about 2.5. Thus a star of the first magnitude is 2.5 times brighter than one of the second magnitude, 6.25 times the third, 16 times the fourth, 40 times the fifth and 100 times the sixth.

Stars classed under one magnitude are not exactly alike in brightness, and fractional magnitudes are used. A few stars and planets are brighter than first magnitude and have magnitudes less than one. The magnitude of Sirius, the brightest star, is -1.4 and that of Venus, the brightest planet, can reach -4.4. This difference of three magnitudes makes Venus sometimes 16 times brighter than Sirius.

The magnitude of Mira is marked "Var.," which means that it varies in brightness. This was the first variable star discovered. Most of the time it can be observed only with a telescope, but at intervals of about eleven months it can be seen with the unaided eye.

Overleaf:

Fig. 2-27. This chart shows the principal stars and constellations from the north celestial pole to 60° south of the celestial equator. The numbers along the equator mark the hours of right ascension. Declination is indicated at intervals of 30° along the four hour lines, 0, 6, 12, and 18.

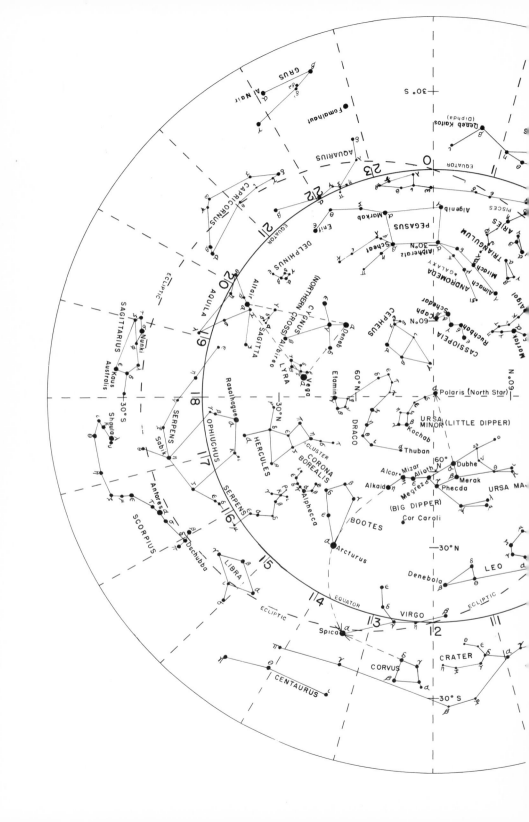

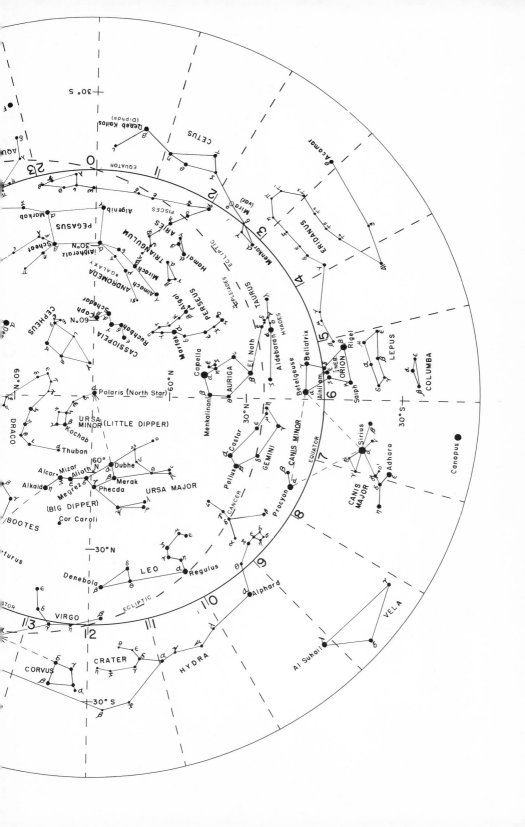

Constellations on Star Chart

	R.A. (Hours)	Dec. (Degrees)
Andromeda	1	+40
Aquarius	22	−10
Aquila	20	0
Aries	2	+20
Auriga	5	+40
Bootes	14	+30
Cancer	9	+20
Canis Major	7	−20
Canis Minor	7	+10
Capricornus	21	−20
Cassiopeia	1	+60
Centaurus	14	−40
Cepheus	22	+70
Cetus	2	−10
Columba	6	−40
Corona Borealis	16	+30
Corvus	12	−20
Crater	11	−10
Cygnus	20	+40
Delphinus	21	+10
Draco	17	+60
Eridanus	4	−30
Gemini	7	+30
Grus	22	−50
Hercules	17	+30
Hydra	11	−10
Leo	11	+20
Lepus	5	−20
Libra	15	−20
Lyra	19	+40
Ophiuchus	17	0
Orion	6	0
Pegasus	0	+20
Perseus	3	+40
Pisces	1	+10
Sagitta	20	+20
Sagittarius	19	−30
Scorpius	17	−30

	R.A. (*Hours*)	Dec. (*Degrees*)
Serpens	16, 18	0
Taurus	5	+20
Triangulum	2	+30
Ursa Major	12	+60
Ursa Minor	15	+80
Vela	9	−50
Virgo	13	0

Finding List of Named Stars on Star Chart

Name	Greek Letter and Constellation	R.A. (*Hours*)	Dec. (*Degrees*)	Mag.
Acamar	Theta Eridani	2.9	−40	2.9
Adhara	Epsilon Canis Majoris	7.0	−29	1.5
Albireo	Beta Cygni	19.5	+28	3.1
Alcor	80 Ursae Majoris	13.4	+55	4.0
Aldebaran	Alpha Tauri	4.6	+16	0.9
Algenib	Gamma Pegasi	0.2	+15	2.8
Algol	Beta Persei	3.1	+41	2.1
Alioth	Epsilon Ursae Majoris	12.9	+56	1.8
Alkaid	Eta Ursae Majoris	13.8	+49	1.9
Almach	Gamma Andromedae	2.0	+42	2.1
Al Nair	Alpha Gruis	22.1	−47	1.8
Alnilam	Epsilon Orionis	5.6	− 1	1.7
Alphard	Alpha Hydrae	9.4	− 9	2.0
Alphecca	Alpha Coronae Borealis	15.6	+27	2.2
Alpheratz	Alpha Andromedae	0.1	+29	2.1
Al Suhail	Lambda Velorum	9.1	−43	2.2
Altair	Alpha Aquilae	19.8	+ 9	0.8
Antares	Alpha Scorpii	16.5	−26	0.9
Arcturus	Alpha Bootis	14.2	+19	−0.1
Bellatrix	Gamma Orionis	5.4	+ 6	1.6
Betelgeuse	Alpha Orionis	5.9	+ 7	0.4

Name	Greek Letter and Constellation	R.A. (Hours)	Dec. (Degrees)	Mag.
Canopus	Alpha Carinae	6.4	−53	−0.7
Capella	Alpha Aurigae	5.2	+46	0.1
Caph	Beta Cassiopeiae	0.1	+59	2.3
Castor	Alpha Geminorum	7.5	+32	1.6
Cor Caroli	Alpha Canum Venaticorum	12.9	+38	2.9
Deneb	Alpha Cygni	20.7	+45	1.3
Deneb Kaitos (Diphda)	Beta Ceti	0.7	−18	2.0
Denebola	Beta Leonis	11.8	+15	2.1
Dschubba	Delta Scorpii	16.0	−23	2.3
Dubhe	Alpha Ursae Majoris	11.0	+62	1.8
El Nath	Beta Tauri	5.4	+29	1.7
Enif	Epsilon Pegasi	21.7	+10	2.3
Etamin	Gamma Draconis	17.9	+51	2.2
Fomalhaut	Alpha Piscis Austrini	22.9	−30	1.2
Hamal	Alpha Arietis	2.1	+23	2.0
Kaus Australis	Epsilon Sagittarii	18.4	−34	1.8
Kochab	Beta Ursae Minoris	14.8	+74	2.0
Marfak	Alpha Persei	3.4	+50	1.8
Markab	Alpha Pegasi	23.1	+15	2.5
Megrez	Delta Ursae Majoris	12.2	+57	3.3
Menkalinan	Beta Aurigae	6.0	+45	1.9
Menkar	Alpha Ceti	3.0	+ 4	2.5
Merak	Beta Ursae Majoris	11.0	+57	2.4
Mira	Omicron Ceti	2.3	− 3	Var.
Mirach	Beta Andromedae	1.1	+35	2.0
Mizar	Zeta Ursae Majoris	13.4	+55	2.0
Nunki	Sigma Sagittarii	18.9	−26	2.1
Phecda	Gamma Ursae Majoris	11.9	+54	2.4
Polaris	Alpha Ursae Minoris	2.0	+89	2.0
Pollux	Beta Geminorum	7.7	+28	1.2

Stars on Star Chart

Name	Greek Letter and Constellation	R.A. (Hours)	Dec. (Degrees)	Mag.
Procyon	Alpha Canis Minoris	7.6	+ 5	0.4
Rasalhague	Alpha Ophiuchi	17.6	+13	2.1
Regulus	Alpha Leonis	10.1	+12	1.4
Rigel	Beta Orionis	5.2	− 8	0.1
Ruchbah	Delta Cassiopeiae	1.4	+60	2.7
Sabik	Eta Ophiuchi	17.1	−16	2.5
Saiph	Kappa Orionis	5.8	−10	2.1
Scheat	Beta Pegasi	23.0	+28	2.5
Schedar	Alpha Cassiopeiae	0.6	+56	2.2
Shaula	Lambda Scorpii	17.5	−37	1.6
Sirius	Alpha Canis Majoris	6.7	−17	−1.4
Spica	Alpha Virginis	13.4	−11	0.9
Thuban	Alpha Draconis	14.0	+65	3.6
Vega	Alpha Lyrae	18.6	+39	0.0

Meanings of Forty Star Names

The commonly used names of the brightest stars have been handed down from early times, being of Arabic, Greek and Latin origin. The ancients generally designated stars by their positions in the constellation figures. Several hundred stars have been given special names, but less than one hundred are in common use today. The following alphabetical list of forty stars is a selection of many of the better-known names.

1. **Aldebaran** (*Alpha Tauri*) is from the Arabic *al dabaran* (the follower), since it is just east of the Pleiades and follows them in the daily westward turning of the sky.

2. **Algol** (*Beta Persei*) is from the Arabic *ras al ghul* (the demon's head), marking the head of Medusa which was cut off by Perseus. Of the same origin is the modern word "ghoul," an evil spirit supposed to rob graves, and by extension, a person who robs dead bodies, graves or the like. Algol is a famous eclipsing double star, which changes in brightness in a period of a little less than three days.

3. **Alkaid** (*Eta Ursae Majoris*). Although many different peoples thought of Ursa Major, the Big Bear, as a bear, the Arabs regarded the four stars forming the bowl of our Big Dipper as a coffin. The stars in the handle of the dipper were considered mourners marching behind the coffin. The last one was called *al kaid banat al nash* (the chief of the mourners). It was once customary to hire mourners at a funeral and it is said that the chief marched at the end of the procession in order to see that the others put on a good show of grief and earned their pay. The complete name for this star would be Alkaid Benetnasch, but only one name or the other is used, usually Alkaid.

4. **Alnilam** (*Epsilon Orionis*) is from the Arabic *al nizam* (the string of pearls) set in the middle of Orion's belt.

5. **Alphecca** (*Alpha Coronae Borealis*) is from *al nair al fakkah* (the bright one of the dish), since in early Arabia this constellation was thought of as a dish. Also, the Persians called it the Broken Platter, because the circle of stars is incomplete. A second name of the star is Gemma, which is the Latin word for bud, referring to the unopened blossoms and leaves of the floral crown.

6. **Alpheratz** (*Alpha Andromedae*) is from the Arabic *al faras* (the

horse), since it was formerly associated with Pegasus. It marks the north-eastern corner of the Square of Pegasus, but for some reason it was trans-ferred to mark the head of Andromeda.

7. **Altair** (*Alpha Aquilae*) means the flying eagle and is from a part of the Arabic name for the constellation of Aquila, the Eagle.

8. **Antares** (*Alpha Scorpii*) is from the Greek *anti* (against, similar to, or rival of) and *Ares* (Greek god of war corresponding to the Roman Mars), so called because this red star resembles the planet Mars in color.

9. **Arcturus** (*Alpha Bootis*) is from the Greek *arktos* (bear) and *ouros* (guard or keeper). It is a part of Bootes, the Bear-Keeper or Bear-Driver. Our word "arctic" means pertaining to or situated under the Bears. The arctic region is that part of the earth where the constellations of the Little Bear and Big Bear appear nearly overhead. In the opposite direction is the antarctic region, where the Bears are always below the horizon.

10. **Betelgeuse** (*Alpha Orionis*) is from the Arabic *ibt al jauzah* (armpit of the central one). It is located in the right shoulder of Orion.

11. **Canopus** (*Alpha Carinae*), according to one derivation is from the name of the chief pilot of the fleet of Menelaus, who stopped in Egypt on his return from the destruction of Troy. The ancient city of Canopus was also named after him. It was the principal port in Egypt for Greek trade before the founding of Alexandria. Canopus, the second brightest star, is used as the guide star for unmanned spacecraft, because of its brightness and its position near the south pole of the ecliptic (the plane of the earth's orbit around the sun).

12. **Capella** (Alpha Aurigae) comes from the Latin and means the little she-goat. It marks the goat which Auriga is holding.

13. **Caph** (*Beta Cassiopeiae*) is from the Arabic title of the constellation, *kaff al hadib* (large hand stained with henna), the bright stars marking the fingertips. Thus the early Arabs had an entirely different figure here, in no way connected with the queen, Cassiopeia.

14. **Castor** (*Alpha Geminorum*) in Greek mythology was the twin brother of Pollux. These stars were favorites of the ancient Romans. When they wished to make a solemn oath, they would swear by Gemini. That is the origin of our expression "by jiminy." The Gemini spacecraft for two astronauts has made the name very familiar.

15. **Cor Caroli** (*Alpha Canum Venaticorum*) was originally known as Cor Caroli Regis Martyris, the Latin for Heart of Martyred King Charles. It was so named in honor of Charles I of England, who was executed in 1649. This is one of the few cases where a fairly modern name relating to a person has become recognized.

16. **Deneb** (*Alpha Cygni*) is from the Arabic *dhanab* (tail), marking the tail of Cygnus, the Swan.

17. **Deneb Kaitos** (*Beta Ceti*) is from *dhanab* (tail) and *kaitos* (whale),

marking the tail of Cetus, the sea monster. A second name for this star is Diphda, which is more commonly used today, although its origin is not related to the name of the constellation. It comes from *al difdi* (the frog).

18. **Denebola** (*Beta Leonis*) is from *dhanab al asad* (tail of the lion).

19. **Dnoces** (*Iota Ursae Majoris*) is the word "Second" spelled backwards and was named in honor of Edward H. White, the Second, who was one of the three astronauts who died in the fire of an Apollo spacecraft during a simulated countdown on January 27, 1967. This star is one of thirty-seven stars used for navigation in the trips to the moon. The stars named in honor of the other two astronauts are Navi and Regor, which are given later in this list.

20. **El Nath** (*Beta Tauri*) is from the Arabic *al natih* (the butting one), marking the tip of the northern horn of Taurus, the Bull.

21. **Fomalhaut** (*Alpha Piscis Austrini*) is from the Arabic *fum al hut* (mouth of the fish), situated in the mouth of the Southern Fish.

22. **Kaus Australis** (*Epsilon Sagittarii*) is from the Arabic *kaus* (bow) and the Latin *australis* (southern), marking the southern part of the bow of Sagittarius, the Archer.

23. **Marfak or Mirfak** (*Alpha Persei*) means elbow in Arabic. The name has been used to designate several different stars, but the one most commonly used today is in Perseus.

24. **Markab** (*Alpha Pegasi*) in Arabic means a saddle, ship, vehicle or anything ridden upon. It marks the southeastern corner of the Square of Pegasus, the Winged Horse.

25. **Mira** (*Omicron Ceti*) is the Latin word for wonderful, named because of its wonderful changes of light. It was the first variable star to be discovered. Most of the time it is visible only with a telescope, but once about every eleven months it is bright enough to be observed without optical aid for a few weeks. It was first recorded by Fabricius in 1596, before the invention of the telescope. Its period of variation was not determined until 1667.

26. **Navi** (*Gamma Cassiopeiae*) is "Ivan" spelled backwards and was named in honor of Virgil Ivan Grissom, one of the three astronauts killed in the Apollo fire. It is the middle star of the "W" of Cassiopeia. See also Dnoces and Regor in this list.

27. **Polaris** (*Alpha Ursae Minoris*) is from the Latin *stella polaris* (pole star), better known as the North Star.

28. **Pollux** (*Beta Geminorum*) in Greek mythology was the twin brother of Castor. These stars mark the heads of Gemini, the Twins. Although Pollux is the brighter of the two, it is named Beta.

29. **Procyon** (*Alpha Canis Minoris*) is from the Greek *pro* (before) and *kyon* (dog), since in latitudes north of 30°N. it rises just before the Dog Star, Sirius.

30. **Rasalhague** (*Alpha Ophiuchi*) is from the Arabic *ras al hawwa* (head of the serpent charmer).

31. **Regor** (*Gamma Velorum*) is "Roger" spelled backwards and was named in honor of Roger B. Chaffee, one of the three astronauts killed in the Apollo fire. See also Dnoces and Navi.

32. **Regulus** (*Alpha Leonis*) is a Latin word meaning a petty king or prince. It is the diminutive of *rex* (king) and the star was so called by Copernicus as the equivalent of an earlier Greek word. The name came from an ancient belief that this star ruled the affairs of the heavens.

33. **Rigel** (*Beta Orionis*) is from the Arabic *rijl* (foot), marking the left foot of Orion.

34. **Shaula** (*Lambda Scorpii*) is probably from the Arabic *shaulah* (sting), marking the sting of the Scorpion. One author believes that the name came from *mushalah* (raised), referring to the position of the sting ready to strike.

35. **Sirius** (*Alpha Canis Majoris*) has been generally thought to come from the Greek *seirios*, which means sparkling or scorching. This word was originally employed to indicate any bright and sparkling star, but gradually became a proper name for the brightest star. Sirius is also known as the "Big Dog Star" or simply the "Dog Star," since it is a part of Canis Major, the Big Dog. Sirius rises at about the same time that the sun does during the second half of July. The ancient Greeks believed that this star had something to do with the hot days of summer. Hence arose the expression "dog days."

36. **Spica** (*Alpha Virginis*) is the Latin word for an ear of wheat or corn. It has come into English unchanged as the name of the star and also as spike. The star marks the spike of grain which Virgo holds.

37. **Vega** (*Alpha Lyrae*) is also spelled Wega and comes from the Arabic *waqi* (falling), that is, the falling vulture. It belongs to Lyra, the Lyre, which was at one time known as Vultur Cadens, the Falling Vulture. The constellation was once pictured as a vulture bearing a lyre in its beak. It formed a group with two other birds, whose names have persisted. They are Cygnus, the Swan, and Aquila, the Eagle. Later the constellation in which Vega is located came to be known as Lyra, but its earlier association with a bird is shown in the name of Vega.

38. **Zubenelgenubi** (*Alpha Librae*) is from the Arabic *al zuban al janubiyyah* (the southern claw), since Libra once marked the claws of the Scorpion.

39. **Zubenelhakrabi** (*Gamma Librae*) is from the Arabic *al zuban al akrab* (the scorpion's claw). See No. 38.

40. **Zubeneschamali** (*Beta Librae*) is from the Arabic *al zuban al shamalijjah* (the northern claw). See No. 38.

These last three names are suggested to parents who wish to name their twins or triplets after stars.

Stories of
the Constellations

The sky is divided into named areas called constellations in much the same way that our country is divided into named areas called states. It is probable that in most cases the ancient stargazers named the constellations in honor of their gods, goddesses, and animals, and not because the groups of stars looked anything like them. Most people think that the constellations are supposed to be pictures, because they bear the names of objects, animals and persons. However, when we look at a map of the United States, we do not expect that the state of Washington will look anything like George.

At some distant time in the past it was thought necessary that a constellation should look like the creature after which it was named. So artists stretched their imagination to the utmost to make pictures that would fit the positions of the stars. In most cases it was a hopeless task, because the stars have usually not been obliging enough to group themselves into the outlines of pictures. To find Pegasus, no person looks for a winged horse. He recognizes it by four stars which form a square. Cassiopeia is supposed to be a lady seated in a chair, but she is found because of her resemblance to a letter "W". Ursa Major means the Big Bear, but how many people find that area in the sky by trying to trace the outline of a bear? Everybody simply looks for the Big Dipper, which is the conspicuous part of Ursa Major.

Although we do not have much use for the outlines of mythological figures, the stories about them are interesting and they help us to locate the constellations with respect to each other. For instance, those who know the story of Andromeda can easily remember the names of the constellations near her. Cassiopeia was her mother and Cepheus was her father. The hero's name was Perseus, who saved Andromeda from Cetus, the sea monster. The winged horse, Pegasus, also entered into the story.

According to one legend, Orion was killed by the sting of Scorpius, the Scorpion. When the two figures were put in the sky, they were put just as far apart as possible so that there would be no further trouble between them. Thus it is easy to remember their relative positions. Orion is at his highest on a winter evening, while Scorpius crosses the meridian in the evening during the summer months. Orion does not dare appear above the horizon until Scorpius has set.

The outlines of the mythological figures and the positions of the principal stars in them are shown in the next five maps. The first is the northern circumpolar map and the others are those of the four seasons. The following constellations are arranged alphabetically. The map on which each one can be found is indicated in parentheses after the name.

Andromeda (Autumn). The story which includes the greatest number of constellations is that of Andromeda. Her mother, Cassiopeia, and her father, Cepheus, are shown on the northern circumpolar map, but the other constellations appear on the autumn map. Cassiopeia boasted that she was more beautiful than the sea nymphs, who became angry and asked Neptune, the god of the sea, to punish her. He did so by sending Cetus, a sea monster, to lay waste the sea coast and to kill the people and cattle living there.

Cepheus consulted an oracle and asked for advice. He was told that the only way to appease the anger of Neptune and the sea nymphs was to sacrifice Andromeda to the sea monster. So she was chained to a rock by the sea to await her fate.

In the meantime Perseus was returning from his triumph over Medusa. This lady, like Cassiopeia, had been too boastful, saying that she was more beautiful than Minerva, the goddess of wisdom. Minerva changed the beautiful hair of Medusa into a coil of snakes and decreed that any person who looked at the face of Medusa would be turned into stone.

Fig. 4-1. Northern circumpolar constellations.

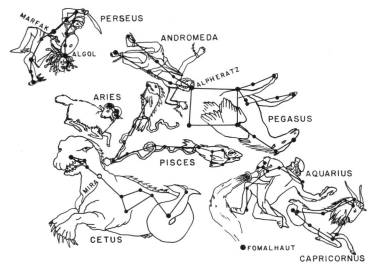

Fig. 4-2. Constellations of autumn.

So many stone statues sprang up that a rather serious traffic problem developed. Finally, Perseus, using his shiny shield as a rear-view mirror and watching Medusa's image in it, backed up to her and cut off her head with his sword. From the blood of Medusa sprang the winged horse Pegasus.

When Perseus found Andromeda about to be devoured by the sea monster, he turned it into stone by exposing it to a view of the face of Medusa, which is marked in the sky by the eclipsing binary star, Algol. Thus Andromeda was saved by Perseus and they lived happily ever after.

Aquarius, the Water Carrier (Autumn). This group has been represented from remote times by the figure of a man pouring water from a jar. He is a symbol of the rainy season, since the rains occurred at the time when the sun was in the direction of this constellation.

This is the middle of a region in the sky called the Sea. Also included are the Fishes, the Southern Fish, the Sea Goat, the Sea Monster, and the River Eridanus.

Aquila, the Eagle (Summer). This was the eagle which carried the thunderbolts of Jupiter. Also it was sent down to earth to find a cupbearer for the gods, bringing back in its claws the handsome Ganymede. The eagle was rewarded by being placed among the constellations.

Ganymede has been associated with Aquarius, but that is a very ancient figure pouring water on the earth and it should not be thought of as a pourer of nectar into the goblets of the gods. However, as an aid to memory, it should be noted that these two constellations, beginning with the same first three letters, adjoin each other, with Aquarius to the southeast of Aquila.

Aries, the Ram (Autumn). The most famous story about this connects it with the expedition of the Argonauts in their search for the Golden Fleece. Phrixus and Helle, the children of Athamas, were badly treated by their stepmother. Mercury sent a golden ram to enable them to escape from her. They were carried on the ram's back through the air, but Helle fell off while they were passing over the strait dividing Europe from Asia. In memory of her fate, this strait was called the Hellespont, but it is now called the Dardanelles.

Phrixus landed safely at the eastern end of the Black Sea. In gratitude to the gods for his rescue, he sacrificed the ram and presented its golden fleece to the king of the country. It was guarded by a dragon which never slept, but was finally carried off by Jason, the leader of the Argonauts.

Auriga, the Charioteer (Winter). This constellation is very ancient, but there is no story which really explains the figure supposedly represented by its stars. Its shape is meaningless and is commonly thought of as a pentagon, although one of the five stars so used really belongs to Taurus. It is always called the Charioteer, but there is no chariot and no horse. Auriga is holding the reins in his right hand, a goat on his left shoulder, and two little kids in his left arm. The goat is marked by Capella, which means the little she-goat. The two kids are marked by a small triangle.

According to one legend, Auriga represents Erechtheus, the lame son of Vulcan. Because of his inability to walk with ease, he invented the chariot and this invention secured for him a place in the celestial Hall of Fame.

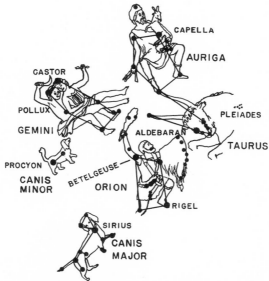

Fig. 4-3. Constellations of winter.

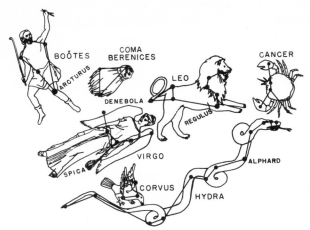

Fig. 4-4. Constellations of spring.

Bootes, the Bear Driver (Spring). Bootes holds in leash the Hunting Dogs, a constellation too faint to be shown in these maps. As the rotation of the earth carries the Big Bear around the North Star, Bootes seems to be pursuing it.

Bootes is also called the herdsman. He was said to have invented the plow and was placed in the sky as a reward.

Cancer, the Crab (Spring). This is one of the faintest constellations in the sky, but its name has become well known because of the Tropic of Cancer. This is the circle on the earth 23½° north of the equator, where the sun is overhead at the time of the summer solstice. About 2,000 years ago the sun was in front of the stars of Cancer at that time of the year. Because of the precession of the equinoxes, the summer solstice has moved westward into Gemini.

Cancer is the Latin word for crab and it has been suggested that this name was given because the peculiar sidelong gait of a crab is like the behavior of the sun when it reaches the solstice.

According to the Greek legend, while Hercules was struggling with Hydra, Juno sent a crab to attack him. The crab bit Hercules, who quickly killed it. Juno then rewarded it by placing it among the stars.

Canis Major, the Big Dog, and Canis Minor, the Little Dog (Winter). These two dogs to the east of Orion are naturally associated with that hunter. Canis Major looks something like a dog, but Canis Minor is composed of only two stars and was probably invented by the Egyptians for a definite purpose.

Sirius, the Big Dog Star, rose just ahead of the sun at the time of the rising of the Nile River each year and enabled them to plan for the inundation. Procyon, the Little Dog Star, rises just before Sirius. Thus the

Egyptians used these two stars as reliable watchdogs, rather than as the hunting dogs of Orion.

Capricornus, the Sea Goat (Autumn). This figure is a Sea Goat, whatever that might be. At one time the winter solstice was in Capricornus. Perhaps the reason that the ancients used the figure of a goat, an expert climber, was that the sun appeared to begin its climb up the sky from its lowest position here. They may have given it the tail of a fish to symbolize the rains of the winter season. Our Tropic of Capricorn, 23½° south of the earth's equator, was so named when the southernmost point of the sun's path was in this constellation.

Cassiopeia (Circumpolar). See Andromeda.

Cepheus (Circumpolar). See Andromeda.

Cetus (Autumn). See Andromeda.

Coma Berenices, Berenice's Hair (Spring). The name of this faint constellation was derived from a story of the third century B.C. Queen Berenice of Egypt was worried about her husband, who had gone off to war. She made a vow that if he returned safely she would cut off her long beautiful hair and consecrate it to the gods in the temple of Venus.

The king finally returned and Berenice, true to her vow, cut off her hair and placed it in the temple. One night the hair disappeared and the guardians of the temple were called on to explain what had happened to it. Conon, the Astronomer Royal, explained that the gods were so pleased with the sacrifice of Berenice that they took her hair and placed it among the stars. This constellation is marked by a faint cluster of stars.

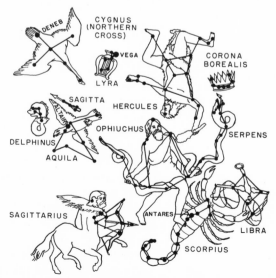

Fig. 4-5. Constellations of summer.

Corona Borealis, the Northern Crown (Summer). This is one of the few constellations which resemble the objects after which they were named. It is called the Northern Crown to distinguish it from Corona Australis, the Southern Crown.

Ariadne was the daughter of Minos, the king of Crete, who kept in a labyrinth the ferocious Minotaur, which was half man and half bull. Each year the Athenians were forced to send seven youths and seven maidens as a tribute to Crete to be devoured by the Minotaur. One year Theseus, the son of King Aegeus of Athens, volunteered to go as one of the victims, hoping to be able to kill the monster.

When the fourteen victims were brought before King Minos, his daughter Ariadne noticed Theseus and immediately fell in love with him. She arranged to see him alone and gave him a sword and a ball of thread. Unwinding the thread as he followed the winding paths of the labyrinth, he came upon the monster and slew it. Then he retraced his steps with the aid of the thread and escaped with his companions, taking Ariadne with him.

On the way home they stopped at the island of Naxos, where Theseus abandoned Ariadne, while she lay sleeping, and he sailed on alone. It is not known why he did this, but one explanation is that he was ordered to do it by the god Bacchus. At any rate Bacchus later took Ariadne to be his wife and gave her a golden crown set with gems. When she died he placed this crown in the heavens.

Corvus, the Crow (Spring). According to a Greek legend, Apollo fell in love with Coronis, but being very jealous, he sent a crow to spy upon her. The crow reported that Coronis was untrue to Apollo, who rewarded the crow by placing it among the stars. Just why Corvus appears to be attacking Hydra in the sky has not been explained.

Cygnus, the Swan (Summer). Various legends relate to this group, which is also called the Northern Cross. It became associated with the swan into which Zeus transformed himself when he was wooing Leda, the wife of the king of Sparta. Also it is concerned with the story of Phaeton, the son of Apollo, which will be briefly told here.

Phaeton did not know who his father was until one day his mother, a mortal, told him. His friends teased him, daring him to prove that his father was divine. He went to Apollo, who promised him he could have any thing he wanted with which to convince his doubting friends. He asked permission to drive the chariot of the Sun for one day. Apollo did not want him to do this, but Phaeton held him to his promise, and permission was finally granted.

Very soon the horses realized that Phaeton was inexperienced and they ran wild. Sometimes the chariot went too high in the sky and the earth below became very cold. In Africa the chariot came so close that the earth was scorched into a great desert and the inhabitants had their skins blackened.

To prevent any further trouble, Jupiter hurled a thunderbolt at Phaeton and sent him falling to the earth. The horses returned to their stables. Phaeton fell into the river Eridanus and his friend Cycnus dove into the water to try to find his body. He swam back and forth, looking like a swan diving for its food. At last the gods took pity on him and changed him into a swan, a form which would always remind them of his efforts on behalf of Phaeton. He was taken to the sky, where we find him as Cygnus. The similarity between the names, Cycnus and Cygnus, seems to be accidental.

Delphinus, the Dolphin (Summer). The story commonly associated with this is about Arion, a famous musician, who had just won a prize in a musical contest. The sailors on the ship on which he was returning home were envious of his fame and planned to kill him and seize the treasures which had been given him by his admirers. Warned in a dream by Apollo of this plot, Arion played his harp and attracted some dolphins. He leaped on the back of one, which brought him safely to shore.

A popular name for this constellation is "Job's Coffin," which is said to have come from the four stars in it which form a diamond, but do not look very much like a coffin.

Draco, the Dragon (Circumpolar). Since dragons were rather common in mythology, it is natural that a number of stories are associated with Draco. There seems to be no agreement as to which dragon is represented by this constellation.

According to one legend, Draco was the monster that guarded the golden apples in the Garden of Hesperides. As his eleventh labor, Hercules is supposed to have killed this dragon in order to obtain the fruit. However, this story conflicts with a legend that Hercules temporarily supported the weight of the heavens while Atlas went to the garden and got the apples from his nieces.

Draco was also said to be the dragon which guarded a sacred spring from which Cadmus was ordered to secure some water. After a great battle he finally killed it and plucked out its teeth, which he sowed in a field. From them many warriors sprang up and engaged in a battle, from which there were only five survivors. They assisted Cadmus in building Thebes, which was known as the City of the Dragon.

Gemini, the Twins (Winter). Northeast of Orion are two bright stars about 4° apart and of nearly the same brilliance. There is no other pair of stars of equal brightness so close together in the northern half of the sky. It is natural that most of the old stories about the adventures of twin heroes have been associated with these stars. They have been known for a long time as Castor and Pollux, after the famous twins of classical mythology, who went on the journey after the Golden Fleece in the ship *Argo*.

Hercules (Summer). There is no more celebrated hero in mythology than Hercules, and yet the constellation bearing his name is quite faint. Six stars in it resemble the outline of a butterfly. Hercules is pictured upside down in the sky, with one foot on the head of Draco and with his head close to that of Ophiuchus. The latter is struggling with Serpens and has one foot on Scorpius. Apparently we see here a symbol of the never-ending warfare between good, represented by Hercules and Ophiuchus, and evil, represented by the dragon, the serpent, and the scorpion.

Hercules possessed high qualities of mind and character as well as great physical strength. Armed with a huge club, he performed the famous "Twelve Labors" and other remarkable deeds too numerous to mention here. Even when he was an infant and still lay in his cradle, he strangled two serpents which Juno sent to destroy him. She was the wife of Jupiter and was always jealous of her husband's love affairs and of the many sons he had by mortal women. Hercules was the son of Jupiter and a mortal named Alcmene.

The death of Hercules was a tragic affair. When he and his wife, Deianira, came to the ford of a river, he placed her on the back of Nessus, a centaur, who carried travelers across for a fee. Instead of taking her to the other side of the stream, Nessus started off with her for the cavern where he lived. Hercules shot the centaur with an arrow. Before dying, the centaur told Deianira that his blood was a love potion which would enable her to retain the love of Hercules.

Later when she became jealous of one of the slave girls of Hercules, she dipped one of his robes in this supposed love potion. However, it was a deadly poison and caused the death of Hercules soon after he put on the robe.

Hydra, the Water Monster (Spring). Hydra was a terrible monster which lived in the water and looked like a large snake. It had nine heads, of which the middle one was immortal. As his second labor, Hercules was commanded to kill Hydra. When he struck off one head, two new ones grew in its place. At last, with the help of his nephew, he burned away the heads, which prevented other heads from growing out. He buried the immortal head under a rock.

For the sake of simplicity the outline of Hydra is always shown on star maps with only one head. This faint constellation is the longest one of all, extending about one-fourth of the way around the sky.

Leo, the Lion (Spring). The first of the twelve labors of Hercules was to kill the Nemean Lion, which was the largest and fiercest lion in the world. It had such a thick and tough skin that no arrow could penetrate it. Hercules grasped the lion by the throat and after a terrific struggle he strangled it to death. Then he always wore the lion's skin as a covering for his own defense in other exploits.

The front part of Leo looks like a sickle and is commonly called that. The tail is marked by Denebola, which is from the Arabic and means the lion's tail.

Libra, the Scales (Summer). This is the only constellation in the zodiac which does not represent an animal. Its history is very doubtful. The names of its two brightest stars are Zubenelgenubi (meaning "Southern Claw") and Zubeneschamali (meaning "Northern Claw"). They indicate that at one time it was a part of Scorpius, the Scorpion.

Libra was regarded as the scales of justice belonging to Astraea, the goddess of justice, who was represented by Virgo. Also at one time the autumnal equinox was located in Libra. Thus it is supposed that the figure of a balance refers to the fact that the days and nights were of equal length when the sun was in front of the stars of Libra.

Lyra, the Lyre (Summer). This constellation represents the lyre which was made by Mercury out of the back of a tortoise and presented to Apollo, who passed it on to his son Orpheus. After a few years, Orpheus lost his wife Eurydice, who died from the sting of a snake. He then entered Hades and so charmed Pluto and all the spirits of the dead with the beautiful music of his lyre that they agreed to restore Eurydice to life. They did so only on condition that Orpheus would not look back at her until he had reached the upper world. Orpheus became impatient when he did not hear his wife following him. When he looked around, he saw her disappearing in the distance. And so he lost her forever.

Ophiuchus, the Serpent Holder, and Serpens, the Serpent (Summer). Ophiuchus is from two Greek words, meaning "holding a serpent," and that is why these two constellations are considered together. He holds the middle of the serpent, with the head to the west of him and the tail to the east.

According to the Greek legend, Ophiuchus represents the great physician Aesculapius, who was so successful in saving lives that Jupiter had to kill him, because Pluto protested against the decrease in the number of souls going to the underworld. The snake as a symbol of medicine seems to have come from its apparent renewal of life by periodic casting off and renewing of its skin. Aesculapius has been pictured in classic art with a staff, about which a serpent is twined, and this is the emblem of medicine even today. Unfortunately, this symbol is often confused with the caduceus of Mercury, which is a wand with a pair of wings at the top and two snakes draped about it. This is the symbol of messengers, since Mercury was the messenger of the gods.

Orion (Winter). Considered the finest constellation in the heavens,

Orion is the subject of a number of stories, only a few of which can be told here. He fell in love with Merope, whose father, King Oenopion, opposed the marriage and found one reason after another for withholding his consent. After performing many tasks required by Oenopion, Orion realized that the king's promises meant nothing and he tried to elope with Merope. The plan was discovered and the king caused Orion's eyes to be put out.

The blind giant wandered about until he came to the forge of Vulcan, who gave him one of his blacksmiths to guide him to the land of the sun. Here Orion faced the rising sun and his sight was restored.

Diana, the goddess of the moon, fell in love with Orion. Her brother, Apollo, the god of the sun, did not like this, because she was neglecting her duty of driving the chariot of the moon across the sky. When Apollo found Orion bathing alone in the sea, he sent his rays on the water so that nothing could be seen of Orion but a dark spot among the waves. Apollo persuaded Diana to shoot an arrow at this, which she did with fateful results. See also Scorpius.

Pegasus, the Winged Horse (Autumn). See Andromeda.

Perseus (Autumn). See Andromeda.

Pisces, the Fishes (Autumn). This is the last of the three constellations of the zodiac associated with water and through which the sun passed during the rainy season. The other two are Capricornus, the Sea Goat, and Aquarius, the Water Bearer.

The Greeks invented a story to account for these fishes. To escape the monster Typhon, Venus and Cupid jumped into the Euphrates River and assumed the forms of fishes.

Sagitta, the Arrow (Summer). This constellation looks something like its name, but it is not known which arrow it is supposed to represent. Among those suggested are the one with which Apollo killed the Cyclops, the one which Hercules used to kill the vulture tormenting Prometheus, and Cupid's Arrow.

Sagittarius, the Archer (Summer). According to Greek legend, Sagittarius represented Chiron, the most celebrated of the centaurs, who were half horses and half men. He had great knowledge of medicine, music, and marksmanship, and he was a noted educator.

Three stars in a curved line suggest the bow which the archer is holding and one star marks the point of the arrow. However, most of the figure is not outlined by any stars.

Scorpius, the Scorpion (Summer). This is the finest constellation of the zodiac and it really looks like a scorpion. The best-known story is that this is the creature sent by Juno to punish Orion for his boastfulness. The sting of the scorpion caused the death of Orion and then these two constellations were placed as far apart as possible, so that there would be no further trouble between them. Orion is the finest constellation of the winter sky and Scorpius is the outstanding one of the summer sky.

Serpens (Summer). See Ophiuchus.

Taurus, the Bull (Winter). Because of the precession of the equinoxes, Taurus marked the position in the sky occupied by the sun on the first day of spring about 5,000 years ago. This was the most important date in the year, marking the time for ploughing and planting. It was New Year's Day for many of the ancient peoples. This part of the sky was marked by a bull, which was supposed to open up the year and plough the long furrow of the sky called the zodiac.

When the Greeks later adopted the Bull, they accounted for only the front of its body being shown by telling a story of Jupiter. He changed himself into a snow-white bull to attract the attention of Europa, Princess of Phoenicia. Delighted by his unusual beauty and tameness, she seated herself on his back. He dashed down to the sea and swam with her all the way to Crete, where he revealed himself as Jupiter and won her for his bride. Europa gave her name to the continent of Europe and the bull was placed in the sky with his head and shoulders showing above water.

Instead of finding Europa on the back of Taurus, we find it marked in the sky by the Pleiades, a famous star cluster which is also called the Seven Sisters. They were the daughters of Atlas, who were pursued by Orion until Jupiter changed them into doves and then into stars, where we still see them being followed by Orion.

The head of Taurus is marked by a group of stars in the shape of a V. At the upper left is Aldebaran, which marks one eye of the Bull. The other stars in the V belong to a star cluster called the Hyades. The relative positions of Orion and Taurus indicate that they are having a battle and that Taurus is getting the worst of it, because one eye which is marked by a faint star, appears to be nearly closed.

Ursa Major, the Big Bear, and Ursa Minor, the Little Bear (Circumpolar). These constellations are best known as the Big Dipper and the Little Dipper, since seven stars in each form a dipper.

Callisto was a beautiful girl with whom Jupiter fell in love. Juno, the wife of Jupiter, became jealous of Callisto and changed her into a bear. Callisto was afraid of the other animals as well as the hunters, but one day she saw her own son Arcas. She rushed toward him to embrace him, but he raised his spear and was about to kill her, not knowing that she was his mother.

Jupiter was looking down from the heavens and saved Callisto by changing her son also into a bear. Then he took them up and placed them in the sky. To explain the very long tails of the bears, it has been suggested that the bears were pulled up into the sky by their tails, which became stretched on such a long journey. Also it has been pointed out that

61

the Little Bear's tail has become still more stretched, because every day he swings around the north celestial pole, to which the end of his tail is fastened.

Virgo, the Virgin (Spring). This constellation has been identified with almost every goddess who had any relation to the earth and with others as well. According to one legend, Virgo represents Astraea, the goddess of justice, who lived among mankind during the Golden and Silver ages. However, with the coming of the Iron Age, they became so wicked that the gods could not remain on the earth. Then she was placed in the sky with the scales of justice lying beside her in Libra.

Another identification is with Ceres, the goddess of the harvest, since the sun appeared in front of Virgo at the time of the harvest. The brightest star in Virgo is Spica and its name means a spike or an ear of wheat or corn, which Virgo holds.

5

Positions of the Planets

All the planets revolve around the sun in the same direction, in nearly circular orbits, and in nearly the same plane. The time required for a planet to make one trip around the sun is called its sidereal period. Suppose that two planets are lined up with the sun like runners who are about to start off on a race. In the case of either of the inner planets, Mercury and Venus, this line-up is called inferior conjunction. As seen from the earth, the planet appears to be joined to the sun. In the case of an outer planet like Mars, the line-up is called opposition, because as seen from the earth the planet appears in the opposite direction from the sun.

In Fig. 5-1, Venus is in inferior conjunction and Mars is in opposition. Since the earth makes a complete circuit of 360° around the sun in 365¼ days, it moves about one degree per day. The exact amount to three decimals is 0°.986. Similarly, if we divide 360° by 224.7 (the number of days in the period of Venus), we find that it moves 1°.602 per day. Also, dividing 360° by 687 (the number of days in the period of Mars), we get 0°.524 for its daily motion.

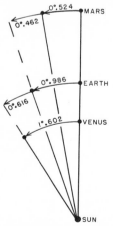

Fig. 5-1. Daily motions
of Venus, earth
and Mars.

These angles have been exaggerated 20 times in Fig. 5-1, to provide enough space to mark them. The amount which Venus gains on the earth in one day is 0°.616. The number of days for Venus to gain a whole lap on the earth is equal to 360° divided by 0°.616. The result is 584 days, which is called the synodic period of Venus. After that interval Venus will again be lined up with the earth and the sun at inferior conjunction.

Similarly, we divide 360° by 0°.462, the earth's daily gain on Mars, and get 780 days as the synodic period of Mars. This is the average interval from one opposition of Mars to the next. Since the orbits of the planets are ellipses, this interval varies. The range in the case of Mars is from about 764 to 810 days.

Venus

In Fig. 5-2 the earth is shown at A and a line AE is drawn tangent to the orbit of Venus at E. Another line, AS, is drawn from the earth to the sun. The angle between these two lines is called the greatest eastern elongation of Venus. It is never more than 48° and averages about 46°. This means that Venus is never seen more than 48° from the sun.

Since AE is tangent to the orbit of Venus (drawn here as a circle), the angle AES is 90° and the angle ESA is 44°. Thus the angles at the earth and at the sun are very nearly equal, and hence AE and ES, the sides of this right triangle, are very nearly equal. Thus at the time of greatest elongation Venus is about equally distant from the earth and the sun.

The interval from greatest eastern elongation to inferior conjunction averages 72 days. During this time the earth moves from A to C and Venus catches up with it in going from E to D. After another 72 days Venus reaches greatest western elongation at W, when the earth is at B.

If the two right triangles, AES and BWS, are swung down so that their hypotenuses, AS and BS, coincide with CS, we have the situation shown in Fig. 5-3. This regards the earth as fixed at C and indicates the relative

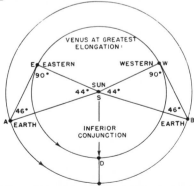

Fig. 5-2. Motions of Venus and the earth from greatest eastern elongation to greatest western elongation.

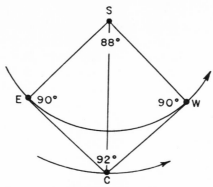

Fig. 5-3. *Venus takes about one-fourth of its synodic period to go from eastern to western elongation.*

positions of Venus with respect to the earth. In going from greatest eastern elongation to greatest western elongation, Venus gains 88° on the earth, as represented by the angle ESW. This is very nearly one-fourth of 360°. Thus the interval required for Venus to go from E to W is about one-fourth of the synodic period, which is the interval required for Venus to gain 360° on the earth.

This synodic period of 584 days is almost exactly equal to 1.6 years, being only about 7½ hours less than that. Therefore, the interval from greatest eastern elongation to greatest western elongation is 0.4 year and the interval from greatest western elongation to greatest eastern elongation is 1.2 years.

Since the greatest elongations are located symmetrically with respect to the conjunctions, they are separated from inferior conjunction by 0.2 year and from superior conjunction by 0.6 year. (*See Fig. 5-4.*)

If we multiply 1.6 by 5, we get 8. Thus Venus completes five synodic periods in eight years. The corresponding configurations of Venus and the earth with respect to the sun repeat themselves on very nearly the same dates every eight years. They come only about 60 (8 times 7½) hours or 2½ days earlier.

Also by various combinations of these three intervals (0.2, 0.6 and 1.6 years) we can get any number of whole years. For example, the intervals from greatest eastern elongation to superior conjunction and from superior conjunction to greatest western elongation each contain two intervals of 0.2 year and one of 0.6 year, making a total of one year.

This is illustrated in Table I, which contains the configurations of Venus from 1977 through 1988. These all occur in the five months of January, April, June, August and November. Examples of the 8-year period between greatest elongations in the same month are from 1977 January 24 to 1985 January 22 and from 1980 April 5 to 1988 April 3.

When Venus is east of the sun, it is an evening star, being visible in the evening above the western horizon. When it is west of the sun, it is a morning star, being visible shortly before sunrise above the eastern horizon. As an aid to memory, it may be helpful to notice that when it is *E*ast of the sun, it is an *E*vening star.

TABLE I

Conjunctions (Superior and Inferior) and Greatest Elongations (Eastern and Western) of Venus (1977–1988)

	January	April	June	August	November
1977	Jan. 24 Eastern	Apr. 5 Inferior	June 15 Western		
1978	Jan. 21 Superior			Aug. 29 Eastern	Nov. 7 Inferior
1979	Jan. 18 Western			Aug. 25 Superior	
1980		Apr. 5 Eastern	June 14 Inferior	Aug. 24 Western	
1981		Apr. 6 Superior			Nov. 10 Eastern
1982	Jan. 21 Inferior	Apr. 1 Western			Nov. 4 Superior
1983			June 16 Eastern	Aug. 25 Inferior	Nov. 4 Western
1984			June 14 Superior		
1985	Jan. 22 Eastern	Apr. 3 Inferior	June 12 Western		
1986	Jan. 18 Superior			Aug. 27 Eastern	Nov. 5 Inferior
1987	Jan. 15 Western			Aug. 22 Superior	
1988		Apr. 3 Eastern	June 12 Inferior	Aug. 22 Western	

For a few weeks around inferior conjunction it appears too close to the sun to be easily observed. In the case of superior conjunction, when Venus is on the far side of the sun, it is hidden from view for several months.

During each synodic period of about 19 months Venus appears too close to the sun to be easily observed for a total of about four months. The remaining 15 months are divided equally between the evening sky and the morning sky. The resulting 7½ months, in the case of the evening star, are composed of about 5½ months before greatest eastern elongation and two months after it. In the case of Venus as a morning star, its visibility extends from about two months before greatest western elongation until about 5½ months after it.

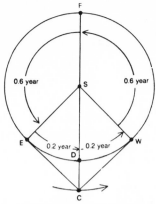

Fig. 5-4. *The circle shows the positions of Venus with respect to the earth (C) and the sun (S) during a synodic period of 1.6 years. The interval from superior conjunction (F) to greatest eastern elongation (E) is three times as long as that from E to inferior conjunction (D). Similarly the interval from greatest western elongation (W) to F is three times as long as that from D to W.*

Mercury

The sidereal period of Mercury is 88 days (about three months) and its synodic period averages 116 days (nearly four months). Since its orbit differs considerably from a circle, its orbital speed varies and its synodic period ranges from 111 to 121 days. Also its greatest elongation varies between 18° and 28°.

As in the case of Venus, Mercury is visible in the evening sky near the western horizon when it is at or near greatest eastern elongation, and is visible in the morning sky near the eastern horizon when it is at or near greatest western elongation. However, in northern latitudes Mercury is never high enough above the horizon to be seen during the hours of darkness. It can be seen only during morning and evening twilight. Also it is visible for only about two weeks around the time of greatest elongation. The most suitable times are when it is an evening star in the spring and when it is a morning star in the autumn. This is due to the changing slant with the horizon of the line connecting Mercury and the sun. (*See Fig. 5-6.*)

Table II lists the greatest elongations of Mercury from 1977 to 1989. Since they repeat themselves on very nearly the same dates every 13 years, later dates can be found by adding 13 years and two or three days to any date in this list. These dates and those used for the other planets have been taken from a series of papers by M. B. B. Heath in the *Journal of the British Astronomical Association* (January, March and April, 1956).

TABLE II
Greatest Elongations of Mercury (1977–1989)

East of Sun (Evening Star)			West of Sun (Morning Star)		
1977	Apr.	10	1977	Jan.	28
	Aug.	8		May	27
	Dec.	3		Sept.	21
1978	Mar.	24	1978	Jan.	11
	July	22		May	9
	Nov.	16		Sept.	4
1979	Mar.	8		Dec.	24
	July	3	1979	Apr.	21
	Oct.	29		Aug.	19
1980	Feb.	19		Dec.	7
	June	14	1980	Apr.	2
	Oct.	11		Aug.	1
1981	Feb.	2		Nov.	19
	May	27	1981	Mar.	16
	Sep.	23		July	14
1982	Jan.	16		Nov.	3
	May	8	1982	Feb.	26
	Sep.	6		June	26
	Dec.	30		Oct.	17
1983	Apr.	21	1983	Feb.	8
	Aug.	19		June	8
	Dec.	13		Oct.	1
1984	Apr.	3	1984	Jan.	22
	July	31		May	19
	Nov.	25		Sep.	14
1985	Mar.	17	1985	Jan.	3
	July	14		May	1
	Nov.	8		Aug.	28
1986	Feb.	28		Dec.	17
	June	25	1986	Apr.	13
	Oct.	21		Aug.	11
1987	Feb.	12		Nov.	30
	June	7	1987	Mar.	26
	Oct.	4		July	25
1988	Jan.	26		Nov.	13
	May	19	1988	Mar.	8
	Sep.	15		July	6
1989	Jan.	9		Oct.	26
	May	1	1989	Feb.	18
	Aug.	29		June	18
	Dec.	23		Oct.	10

Fig. 5-5 shows positions of the earth and Mercury when minimum and maximum values of greatest elongation can occur. The mean distance of Mercury from the sun is 36,000,000 miles, but the eccentricity of its orbit is so great (0.206) that the sun is 7,400,000 miles out of the center. The distance from the sun ranges from 28,600,000 miles at perihelion to 43,400,000 at aphelion.

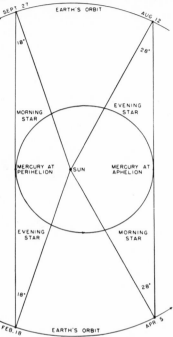

Fig. 5-5. The greatest elongation of Mercury ranges from 18° to 28°, because the eccentricity of its orbit is large.

In Fig. 5-5 lines have been drawn tangent to Mercury's orbit at perihelion and aphelion. The perihelion line intersects the earth's orbit at positions occupied by the earth on about February 18 and September 27. Lines from the earth to the sun make an angle of 18° with the earth-Mercury lines. This is the minimum value of greatest elongation. Mercury is an evening star when it is at perihelion on February 18, since it is east of the sun. It is a morning star at perihelion on September 27, since it is then west of the sun.

The tangent to Mercury's orbit at aphelion intersects the earth's orbit at positions occupied by the earth on about April 5 and August 12. The elongation of Mercury reaches its greatest possible value of 28° at these times, a morning star on April 5 and an evening star on August 12. Within a period of two or three months centered on each of these dates the elongation is within about one degree of the maximum.

From what has been said so far one might think that the most favorable times to see Mercury would be as a morning star in April and as an eve-

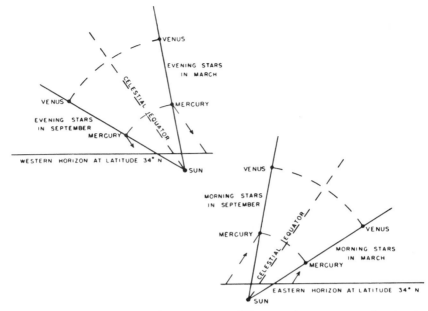

Fig. 5-6. *In the northern hemisphere, Mercury and Venus are best seen as evening stars in March and as morning stars in September. In the southern hemisphere, they are best seen as evening stars in September and as morning stars in March.*

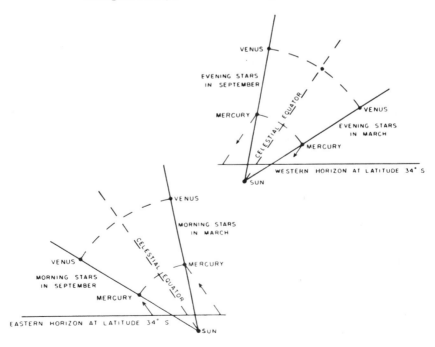

ning star in August. However, there is another important factor which affects the visibility of Mercury.

If the earth's equator were in the plane of the earth's orbit around the sun, the sun would always appear on the celestial equator. Also the planets would always appear on or near the celestial equator, since their orbits are nearly in the same plane. However, since the earth's equator is tilted 23½° to its orbit, the sun appears to describe a circle called the ecliptic, which is inclined 23½° to the celestial equator. The planets always appear on or near the ecliptic.

At any given latitude the celestial equator always makes the same angle with the horizon, which it meets at the east and west points. This angle equals 90° minus the latitude. Thus the celestial equator is perpendicular to the horizon at the earth's equator and inclined 51° to it at Washington, D.C., whose latitude is 39°N. However, as the earth rotates, different parts of the ecliptic make different angles with the horizon.

In the first part of Fig. 5-6 the sun is shown just below the western horizon at the latitude of Atlanta, Georgia, 34°N. As one faces toward the western horizon, south is to the left and north is to the right. The nearly vertical line to the right is part of the ecliptic which is north of the celestial equator. This is the way the ecliptic would appear on March 21, since the sun crosses the celestial equator going northward on that date. Mercury and Venus are shown nearly vertically above the sun at greatest eastern elongation in March.

The other heavy line from the sun slanting to the left represents that part of the ecliptic which would be near the western horizon at sunset on about September 23, when the sun crosses to the south side of the celestial equator. Mercury and Venus are shown at greatest eastern elongation in September. It is obvious that the planets are higher in the sky in March than in September. Arrows indicate how Mercury remains above the horizon a longer time after sunset in March than in September.

The diagram shows Mercury at the same distance from the sun in both cases. Even if it were only 18° from the sun on March 21, it would be higher in the sky at sunset than if it were 28° from the sun on September 23. Therefore, the most favorable time to see Mercury as an evening star in the northern hemisphere is around March 21.

The second part of Fig. 5-6 shows the planets as morning stars above the eastern horizon. In this case they are higher in September than in March. So the best time to see them in the morning sky in the northern hemisphere is around September 23.

It will be noticed that these statements have been qualified with the words "in the northern hemisphere," because the conditions are reversed in the southern hemisphere. The lower diagrams in Fig. 5-6 show the situation at the latitude of Sydney, Australia, 34°S., where the celestial equator is tilted toward the north. The lower left diagram is like the upper left one, except that the celestial equator and the two parts of the ecliptic have been tilted over to the north (right) by 68°, the difference in latitude of 34°N and 34°S. Therefore, in the southern hemisphere the best time to see Mercury and Venus as evening stars is in September. Similarly the best time to see them as morning stars is in March.

It will be recalled that the maximum value of Mercury's greatest elongation as an evening star occurs about August 12. This date is close to September 23, when observers in the southern hemisphere get the greatest advantage from the angle of the ecliptic with the western horizon. Thus the two main factors affecting the favorability of seeing Mercury are present at about the same time in southern latitudes. This makes it possible to see Mercury after dark. This is not true in the northern hemisphere, where the planet can be seen only in twilight.

Similarly the maximum value of Mercury's greatest elongation as a morning star occurs about April 5. This date is close to March 21, when observers in the southern hemisphere get the greatest advantage from the angle of the ecliptic with the eastern horizon. So it is possible in southern latitudes to see Mercury rising in the east before the beginning of morning twilight.

Mars

Since Mars takes nearly two years to revolve around the sun and the earth requires only one year, the interval necessary for the earth to gain one lap on Mars is a little over two years. If the orbits of the planets were concentric circles with the sun at their center, the earth would always pass Mars at the same distance from it and at exactly regular intervals. However, the distance between the elliptical orbits of these two planets ranges from 35 million to 63 million miles and the synodic period varies from about 25 to 27 months.

The two closest approaches of the earth to Mars in recent times occurred in 1956 and 1971. Fig. 5-7 shows the oppositions of Mars during this 15-year interval, with the distances between the planets marked in millions of miles.

Fig. 5-7 also illustrates how the axes of rotation of the two planets are tipped. The orbit of Mars is in nearly the same plane as that of the earth, which is the plane of the diagram. We are looking at the north poles of the planets. Their axes are not pointed straight at us, that is, they are not at right angles to the plane of their orbits.

The tilts of the axes happen to be very nearly the same, the earth's

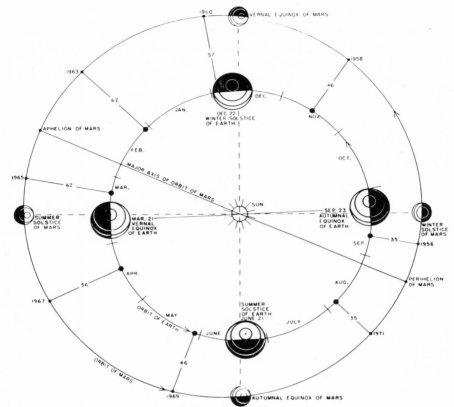

Fig. 5-7. The oppositions of Mars from 1956 to 1971. Distances of Mars from the earth are in millions of miles. The two planets are shown (much enlarged) at their four seasonal positions.

being 23½° and that of Mars about 25°. However, the axes are not pointed in the same direction. The earth's axis is pointed very nearly at the North Star, while the axis of Mars is pointed at a spot in the sky about 35° away from the North Star.

A horizontal dashed line connects the positions of Mars at its two solstices. All the seasons marked in the diagram refer to the northern hemispheres of the two planets. The summer solstice of Mars is at the left, where its north pole is tipped toward the sun. The winter solstice is at the right, where the north pole is tipped away from the sun. A vertical dashed line connects the positions of Mars at its two equinoxes.

The four seasonal positions of the earth lie very close to those of Mars, but they are shifted by one season. The line joining the equinoxes of the earth nearly coincides with the line connecting the solstices of Mars, the two being inclined to each other by only about two degrees. Whenever the earth is passing Mars, the seasonal date on Mars is one season ahead of that on the earth. Thus when Mars is in opposition on September 28, 1988, that will be just a few days after the autumnal equinox on the earth and the beginning of winter in the northern hemisphere of Mars.

At that time Mars will be 37 million miles from the earth, making it the closest approach since 1971. This is shown in the upper part of Fig. 5-8, which includes all the oppositions from 1956 to 1988. The dates from 1956 to 1971 are marked close to the sun, and those from 1973 to 1988 are marked just inside the earth's orbit.

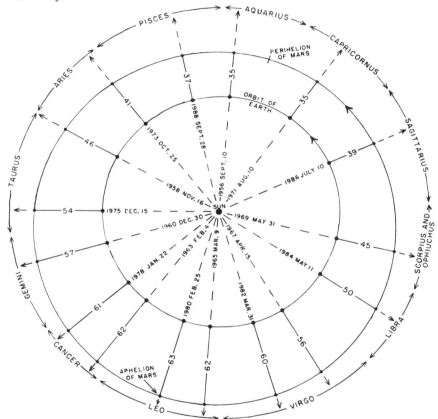

Fig. 5-8. Oppositions of Mars from 1956 to 1988.

The names lying on a circle on the outside of Fig. 5-8 indicate the directions of the constellations in which Mars appears at the different oppositions. Although there are only twelve constellations in the zodiac, a planet can sometimes be within the area of a neighboring constellation when it is a few degrees from the ecliptic (the plane of the earth's orbit). In fact, a part of the ecliptic about 18° long lies within the boundaries of

Ophiuchus, which is not one of the constellations of the zodiac. The part of the ecliptic within the boundaries of Scorpius is only 7° long. So these two constellations are grouped together to make one of the twelve divisions of the zodiac.

Jupiter

The sidereal period of Jupiter is 11.86 years. During one year it moves about 1/12 of the way around the zodiac, or about 30°. Since the earth moves about 1° per day, it overtakes Jupiter a little over 30 days later from one year to the next. Its synodic period is 398.88 days, or 33.63 days more than one year.

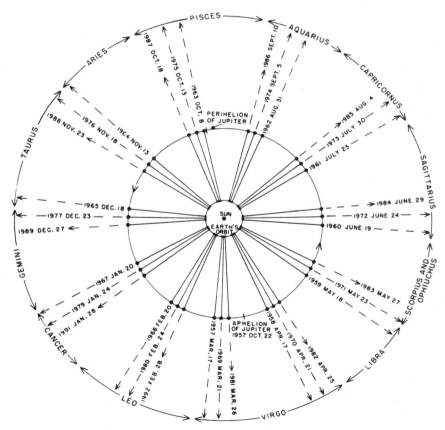

Fig. 5-9. Oppositions of Jupiter from 1957 to 1992.

Eleven synodic periods equal 4,387.68 days, and 12 years equal 4,383 days. The difference between these is 4.68 days. Therefore, the dates of Jupiter's oppositions very nearly repeat themselves every 12 years, coming only 4 or 5 days later. This is brought out in Fig. 5–9, which gives the positions and dates of all oppositions from 1957 through 1992.

Fig. 5–9 contains 33 oppositions of Jupiter, divided into eleven groups of 3 each. The average interval from a date in one group to the corresponding date in the next group is one year and about 34 days. The middle date of each group is halfway between the other two dates in that group, being separated from each one by 12 years plus 4 or 5 days.

Saturn

The sidereal period of Saturn is 29.46 years. Since it moves about 1/30 of the way around the sun or 12° in one year, the earth overtakes it about 13 days later from one year to the next. Fig. 5-10 gives the oppositions of Saturn from 1957 to 1986.

Since Jupiter goes around the sun in about 12 years, it moves eastward among the stars about 30° each year. Thus it gains about 18° on Saturn each year. By dividing 18° into 360°, we find that it gains a lap on Saturn in 20 years. When these planets appear closest together at intervals of about 20 years, they are said to be in conjunction. Although this term implies literally that they are joined together or in the same direction in space, Jupiter does not pass directly in front of Saturn, because their orbits do not lie in the same plane as the earth's orbit.

The last conjunction of these two planets occurred in 1961 and the next one will occur in 1981. In fact, it will be a triple conjunction, like the one which occurred in 1940–1941. As seen from the sun, there can be only a single conjunction, but if the earth is within about 30° of the line joining Jupiter and Saturn in space, when that line passes through the sun, we see a triple conjunction from the moving earth. This occurs, on the average, every 120 years.

In 1940 Jupiter and Saturn were in conjunction on August 15. Then as the earth overtook them, they appeared to move backward or westward among the stars. Jupiter's apparent backward motion, being faster than Saturn's, brought them in conjunction again on October 11. Then as they resumed their eastward motions, Jupiter passed Saturn for the last time on February 20, 1941. In 1981 two conjunctions will occur close together early in the year and the third will follow several months later.

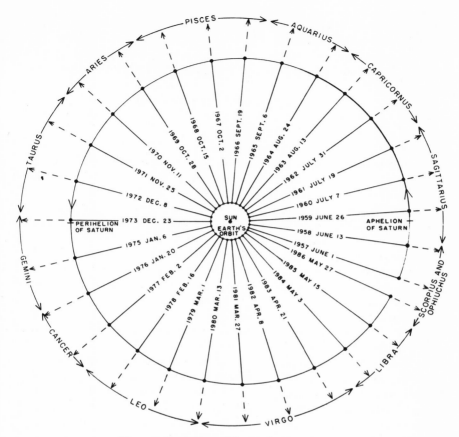

Fig. 5-10. *Oppositions of Saturn from 1957 to 1986.*

The Retrograde Motions
of the Planets

Those who have attended a planetarium show, during which a "year" of planetarium time may pass in a few minutes of ordinary time, know how the planets swing back and forth in their courses among the stars. Most of the time a planet appears to move eastward in what is called direct motion. At intervals it appears to stop and then move westward or backward in what is called retrograde motion. Again it appears to stop and resume its eastward motion, thus progressing around the sky in a series of loops.

The looped paths of the planets were known to the ancients, who had trouble in explaining them because they thought that the earth was fixed and at the center of the universe. The early Greek astronomers worked out a plan which came to be known as the Ptolemaic theory, named from Ptolemy, who lived in the second century A.D. and described the theory in his book, the *Almagest.*

In the Ptolemaic theory each of the five planets known at that time circled around the earth. The small circle on which the planet was supposed to move was called the epicycle. Its center was called the fictitious planet, and the large circle on which it moved around the earth was the deferent. The sun revolved around the earth in a slightly eccentric circle, with the deferents of Mercury and Venus within the sun's orbit and the others outside it. As time went on, many more epicycles were added to make the observations fit better. Still the system did not predict satisfactorily the places of the planets in the sky very far ahead.

In the sixteenth century Copernicus showed how very simply the looped paths of the planets could be explained by placing the sun at the center and having all the planets revolve around it in circles with uniform speeds. For example, the earth moves faster than Mars and overtakes it about every two years. When the earth is passing it, Mars appears to shift backward against the more distant background of stars. It is the same effect which one gets as he drives along in a car and overtakes another car. The latter seems to move backward against the landscape.

The situation is illustrated in Fig. 6-1, where the orbits of Mars and the earth are shown at the bottom and the apparent path of Mars in the sky is marked at the top. The vertical line in the center from the sun through the two planets indicates their positions when Mars is in opposition. At

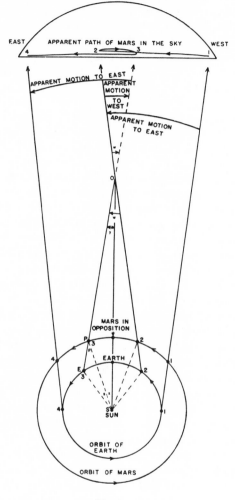

EAST APPARENT PATH OF MARS IN THE SKY WEST

APPARENT MOTION TO EAST

APPARENT MOTION TO WEST

APPARENT MOTION TO EAST

MARS IN OPPOSITION

EARTH

SUN

ORBIT OF EARTH

ORBIT OF MARS

Fig. 6-1.

this time Mars appears opposite the sun in the sky and it is closest to the
earth. Four other positions of each of the planets are marked. Position 1 is
three months before opposition and position 4 is three months after opposition. It is seen that while the earth is going halfway around the sun in
six months, Mars is going only about one-fourth of the way around. The
period of Mars is nearly twice that of the earth.

79

Lines connecting the earth and Mars in their corresponding positions in their orbits indicate the direction of Mars as seen from the earth. All the planets revolve around the sun in an easterly direction, which is counterclockwise in the diagram, if we assume that the north side of the earth is toward us. The general direction of a planet's motion in the sky is also to the east, as shown by the shift of Mars at the top of the diagram from position 1 to position 4. This is from right to left, which is from west to east on a map of the sky.

The eastward motion of Mars in the sky is interrupted between positions 2 and 3, where it appears to be moving westward. The reason for this can be seen by looking at the portions of the planets' orbits between positions 2 and 3. The planets are moving in nearly the same direction. Since the earth is going faster to the left in the diagram than Mars is, the direction of Mars as seen from the earth is shifting to the right.

As the earth revolves around the sun, it causes the sun to appear to trace out a circle in the sky called the ecliptic. If the orbits of the other planets were exactly in the same plane with the earth's orbit, their apparent motions with respect to the stars would be simply forward and backward along the ecliptic. Since the orbits of the other planets are slightly inclined to the plane of the earth's orbit, their paths form loops when the planets are retrograding.

The eastward or direct motion of a planet exceeds the westward or retrograde motion, both in the number of degrees passed over and in the time spent in this motion. There are considerable differences among the planets in the amount of retrograde motion. To find out how many days a planet is retrograding and how far it moves westward in the sky, we can arrive at average values which are approximately correct by assuming that the planets move at constant speeds in circular orbits in the same plane. Actually each planet moves in an ellipse with a varying speed, but the assumption of circular orbits will not affect the results very much and will make the problem much easier to solve.

The interval required for Mercury or Venus to gain a lap on the earth or for the earth to gain a lap on an outer planet is called the planet's synodic period. It is the interval between succeeding inferior conjunctions of an inner planet and the interval between succeeding oppositions of an outer planet. The table lists the synodic period of each planet in days, the number of days of retrograde motion, and the percentage of the total time spent by each planet in retrograding. The last column lists the number of degrees which each planet appears to move westward in the sky during its retrograde motion.

It will be noticed that the farther away a planet is from the earth, the greater is the percentage of time it spends in retrograding. Venus, the

Planet	Synodic Period in Days	Retrograde Interval in Days	% of Time Retrograding	Degrees of Retrograding
Mercury	116	23	20%	13°.4
Venus	584	42	7	16°.6
Mars	780	73	9	16°.2
Jupiter	399	121	30	10°.0
Saturn	378	138	37	6°.8
Uranus	370	152	41	4°.0
Neptune	367	158	43	2°.8
Pluto	367	162	44	2°.4

nearest planet to the earth, has a percentage of 7, while Pluto, the most distant planet, has one of 44. Also the number of degrees of retrograding decreases as the distance from the earth increases. Venus moves westward the most, 16°.6, while Pluto moves the least, 2°.4.

It might be expected that Venus would move westward for a longer time and for a greater distance than it does, since it swings from about 45° east of the sun to the same distance west of the sun. However, most of this change is due to the sun's apparent eastward motion being greater than that of Venus. There is an interval of 144 days from greatest eastern elongation to greatest western elongation. Its western motion with respect to the stars, however, lasts only 42 days.

The chief reason for the apparent complexity of the planetary motions which have been described here is that we are living on one of the revolving planets. We are moving around the sun at the speed of 18½ miles a second. The other planets have different speeds, ranging from 30 miles a second for Mercury to 3 miles a second for Pluto. The speed of a planet is inversely proportional to the square root of its distance from the sun. Pluto, which is at a distance of 40 astronomical units, is 100 times farther from the sun than Mercury, which is at a distance of 0.4 astronomical unit. Therefore, the speed of Pluto is one-tenth the speed of Mercury.

If we could observe the planets from the sun, their motions would appear very simple and orderly. However, in spite of the difficulties made by the motion of our observing platform, a true picture of the solar system was arrived at nearly four centuries ago as a result of the work of Copernicus, Tycho, and Kepler. Later, Newton showed through the law of gravitation why the planets move as they do.

The Apparent Sizes and Magnitudes of the Planets

The brightness of a planet as seen from the earth depends on its size, reflecting power, phase, distance from the sun, and distance from the earth. Since there are considerable ranges in some of these quantities, there are great differences in the amounts of light received by the earth from the planets. When at its brightest, Venus, the nearest planet to the earth, appears about 63,000,000 times brighter than Pluto, the most distant planet, when it is farthest away.

Not only are there differences from one planet to another, but also in several cases there are surprising changes in apparent size and brightness of a planet. For example, when Mars is at its very closest to the earth its apparent diameter is seven times greater than when it is farthest away.

The greatest change in brightness occurs with Mercury. As it revolves around the sun, it turns different portions of its lighted side toward the earth, going through the same phases which the moon does. Fig. 7-1 shows Mercury at three positions in its orbit with respect to the earth and the sun. It is in conjunction when it is in line with the sun and the earth. When it is on the far side of the sun, it is in superior conjunction and is turning all of its lighted side toward the earth.

Since the orbit of Mercury is inclined 7° to the orbit of the earth. Mercury usually does not pass directly behind the sun. Although it is difficult to observe at or near superior conjunction, because of the brilliance of the nearby sun, the planet has been seen with moderate sized telescopes within a few degrees of the sun.

The second position of Mercury shown in Fig. 7-1 is called greatest eastern elongation, when it is farthest separated from the sun as seen from the earth. The angle between the sun and Mercury at this time averages about 23°, varying between 18° and 28° because of the elliptical orbit of Mercury. The phase is like that of the moon at first quarter. Thus we see only half a circle of light, but the apparent size of the planet is larger because it is nearer the earth.

The distance of Mercury from the earth at superior conjunction is about 1½ times that at greatest elongation. Therefore, the angular diameters differ in the same ratio. Since the area is proportional to the square of the diameter, the apparent area of Mercury at greatest elongation is about 9/4

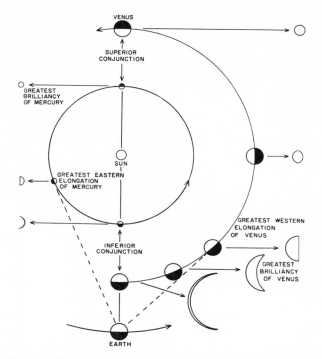

Fig. 7-1. Changing phases and apparent sizes of Mercury and Venus.

that at superior conjunction. Dividing this by 2, because of the half-Mercury phase, we get 9/8. We should expect the planet to appear brighter because of this larger area. However, there must be the same effect here as in the case of the moon.

The half-moon, though apparently of half the area of the full moon, is only one-ninth as bright. This is partly due to the fact that along the dividing line between day and night on the moon the sun's rays strike the surface very obliquely and illuminate it feebly. However, most of the difference must be caused by the roughness of the moon's surface. Except at the full phase, there are shadows cast by the mountains and all the other irregularities. Even the small shadows cast by boulders and pebbles are important, because there are so many of them.

The surface of Mercury is irregular and rough, explaining the apparent contradiction between the brightness at the full phase and at the half phase. Although the apparent area of Mercury is greater at the half phase, the brightness is considerably greater at the full phase.

The third position of Mercury shown in Fig. 7-1 is inferior conjunction, when it is between the earth and the sun. Because of the inclination of its orbit to that of the earth, Mercury usually does not go directly in front of the sun. About 13 times in a century it crosses the sun's disk. This is called a transit.

Unless Mercury is in transit, when it appears as a small, black dot against the sun's disk, it presents a very thin crescent at inferior conjunction. At this time it can appear about 150 times fainter than at superior conjunction. When Mercury is at its brightest, its magnitude is -1.9, and when at its faintest, the number is $+3.5$. The difference of 5.4 magnitudes corresponds to nearly 150 times in brightness.

The right side of Fig. 7-1 shows five positions of Venus with respect to the earth and the sun. It goes through the same phases which Mercury does, but its apparent size changes much more. Its distance from the earth varies from 25 million miles to 162 million miles and so its angular diameter changes by about 6½ times. However, its brightness changes comparatively little, because decreasing apparent size is approximately offset by increasing phase.

Except at the rare event of a transit of the sun, none of which occurs in the twentieth century, Venus shows a large, thin crescent at inferior conjunction. Its magnitude is then about -3.0. When it is at superior conjunction, it presents a small, fully illuminated disk, and its magnitude is about -3.5. Thus it is only about 1.6 times brighter when full than when at the smallest crescent phase.

The greatest brilliancy of Venus is reached about 36 days before and after inferior conjunction. The second of these is shown in Fig. 7-1 as a thick crescent. At this time it can reach a magnitude of -4.4, when it is nearly 2½ times brighter than at the full phase. It is then 16 times brighter than Sirius, the brightest star. Venus is so brilliant that it can be seen with the naked eye in the daytime.

A study of the changes in brightness of Venus at different phases shows that its reflecting surface is much smoother than in the cases of Mercury and the moon. Venus is completely covered with clouds, so that there is not the same darkening at the half phase by the shadows of mountains and other irregularities which exist on the reflecting surfaces of Mercury and the moon.

If the orbits of the planets were circles with the sun at the center of all of them, the brightness of a planet at any particular position with respect to the earth and the sun would always be the same. However, the orbits are ellipses, with the sun located at one focus. The eccentricity of an ellipse is a measure of how much it differs from a circle. Mercury's orbit has the second largest eccentricity of the orbits of the nine major planets. Its value is 0.2 and that of Pluto is 0.25.

The distance of Mercury from the sun varies from 29 million miles at perihelion (nearest the sun) to 43 million miles at aphelion (farthest from the sun). The mean distance (the average of these two figures) is 36 million miles. Multiplying 36 million miles by 0.2, the eccentricity, we get about 7 million miles, which is the amount the distance varies either side of the mean. The eccentricity of the earth's orbit is only 0.017, so that its distance from the sun varies only 1½ million miles on either side of the mean distance of 93 million miles.

Fig. 7-2 shows how the distance of Mercury from the earth varies. If Mercury happens to be at aphelion around June 8 (top of the diagram), its distance from the earth is only 51 million miles. This is found by subtracting the Mercury-sun distance of 43 million miles from the earth-sun distance of 94 million miles. The earth is at its greatest distance of 94½ million miles from the sun on about July 4.

If Mercury happens to be at perihelion around December 9 (bottom of the diagram), its distance from the earth is 63 million miles. This is found by subtracting the Mercury-sun distance of 29 million miles from the earth-sun distance of 92 million miles. Thus we see that when Mercury is at inferior conjunction, its distance from the earth varies from 51 to 63 million miles.

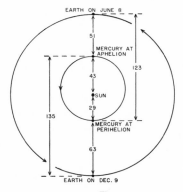

Fig. 7-2. The distance of Mercury from the earth varies from 51 million miles to 135 million miles.

In the case of superior conjunction, we add the distances of the two planets from the sun. The maximum value occurs when Mercury is at aphelion and the earth is at its December 9 position. It is equal to 135 (92 + 43) million miles. The minimum value occurs on June 8 and is equal to 123 (94 + 29) million miles.

With Mercury's distance from the earth varying from 51 million miles at the closest inferior conjunction to 135 million miles at the farthest superior conjunction, it is obvious that its apparent size must vary in the same proportion. The apparent size of a planet is measured by its angular diameter, which is expressed in seconds of arc. For Mercury, the extreme values are 12″.2 and 4″.6.

Mercury appears brightest at superior conjunction, when it is at the full phase, but this brightness varies with its distance from the sun and from the earth. Its greatest brilliancy occurs when it is at perihelion and in superior conjunction at the same time. This is on June 8. Its magnitude is then −1.9, which makes it brighter than any star. Of course, it can be seen only with a telescope then, because of the brilliance of the nearby sun. The data for the different positions of Mercury shown in Fig. 7-2 are summarized in Table III.

TABLE III

Conjunction	Date	Distance (Millions of Miles)	Angular Diameter	Magnitude
Aphelion				
Inferior	June 8	51	12″.2	+3.5
Perihelion				
Inferior	Dec. 9	63	9 .9	+2.8
Perihelion				
Superior	June 8	123	5 .1	−1.9
Aphelion				
Superior	Dec. 9	135	4 .6	−0.8

The orbits of the earth, Mars, Jupiter, and Saturn are shown in Fig. 7-3. Mars has the most eccentric orbit of these four, its eccentricity being 0.093. Its mean distance is 142 million miles, so that its distance from the sun varies by 13 million miles on either side. At aphelion Mars is 155 (142 + 13) million miles from the sun and 63 (155 − 92) million miles from the earth's orbit. At perihelion Mars is 129 (142 − 13) million miles from the sun and 35 (129 − 94) million miles from the earth's orbit.

Since Mars takes about two years to go around the sun, the earth passes it every two years. At such times Mars is in the opposite direction from the sun and is said to be in opposition.

When Mars is at conjunction, its distance from the earth varies from 249 (155 + 94) million miles to 221 (129 + 92) million miles. Thus the extreme range in its distance from the earth is from 35 million miles at the most favorable opposition to 249 million miles at the most distant conjunction. The ratio of these two numbers is 7. Thus its angular diameter varies by 7 times, from 25″.1 to 3″.5.

It will be of interest to see how much the brightness of Mars changes. This varies inversely as the square of the planet's distance from the sun and inversely as the square of the planet's distance from the earth. For example, if a planet at one time were twice as far from the sun as at another,

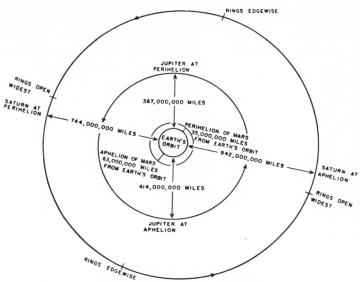

Fig. 7-3. The orbits of the earth, Mars, Jupiter, and Saturn.

it would receive only one-fourth as much light from the sun. That change alone would make the planet appear 4 times fainter. If at the same time the planet's distance from the earth increased by 3 times, that change would make the planet appear 9 times fainter. Multiplying 4 by 9, we find that the two changes would produce a total change of 36 times in the brightness of the planet.

In the case of Mars, its distance from the sun varies from 155 to 129 million miles. Dividing the square of 155 by the square of 129, we get a result of 1.44. The distance of Mars from the earth varies from 249 to 35 million miles. Dividing the square of 249 by the square of 35, we get 50.61. Multiplying this result by 1.44, we find that the range in brightness of Mars is about 73 times. This corresponds to 4.7 magnitudes, Mars changing in magnitude from +2.0 to −2.7.

When Mars is about 90° from the sun in the sky, it shows a phase about like the moon three days from the full. However, at conjunction and at opposition it appears full, and so we do not need to consider the effect of phase on brightness at these positions.

Jupiter's mean distance is 484 million miles and the eccentricity of its orbit is 0.048. Its distance from the sun varies by 23 million miles on either side of the mean, so that the range is from 461 to 507 million miles. Its distance from the earth varies from 367 to 600 million miles, and its magnitude from −2.5 to −1.2.

Saturn's mean distance is 887 million miles and the eccentricity of its orbit is 0.056. Multiplying these two numbers, we get nearly 50 million, so that Saturn's distance from the sun varies by nearly 100 million miles, which is more than the earth's distance from the sun.

The changes in the brightness of Saturn are complicated by the position of the plane of its rings with respect to the earth. When the rings are edgewise to the earth, they are not visible. However, when the rings are most widely displayed, they reflect to us about 1⅔ times as much light as the ball. Fig. 7-3 shows that this phase occurs near the planet's perihelion and aphelion.

When Saturn is at its greatest possible brilliancy its magnitude is −0.3. When the rings are edgewise and the planet is near its most distant point from the earth, the magnitude is about +1.5.

Since Saturn's rings have a real diameter about twice that of Jupiter and since Saturn is about twice as far from the sun as Jupiter, the angular diameter of the rings is about the same as the angular diameter of Jupiter. In fact, when these two planets are nearest the earth, the rings and the polar diameter of Jupiter are exactly equal, having a value of 46″.6.

The brightness of the rings also changes with the phase angle, which is the angle at the planet between lines to the earth and to the sun. When

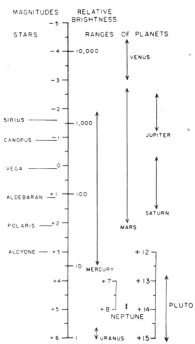

Fig. 7-4. Ranges in brightness of the planets, with the magnitudes of a few stars for comparison.

TABLE IV

	Maximum Magnitude	Minimum Magnitude	Difference in Magnitude	Ratio of Brightness
Mercury	−1.9	+3.5	5.4	145
Venus	−4.4	−3.0	1.4	3.6
Mars	−2.7	+2.0	4.7	73
Jupiter	−2.5	−1.2	1.3	3.2
Saturn	−0.3	+1.5	1.8	5.3
Uranus	+5.7	+6.1	0.4	1.5
Neptune	+7.8	+8.0	0.2	1.2
Pluto	+12.8	+15.1	2.3	8.5

the earth is exactly in line between the sun and Saturn, each particle in the rings hides its own shadow and the entire surface of the rings appears bright. However, when the earth is slightly out of line, the shadow of each particle begins to come out from behind it. Thus the many small shadows decrease the brightness. Since Saturn is about ten times farther from the sun than the earth, the phase angle can never be more than about 6°. Nevertheless, the rings appear about 35% fainter at this very small phase angle than when the angle is 0°.

Of the three telescopic planets, Pluto has the greatest range in magnitude, because its orbit is so eccentric. Uranus has a magnitude of about 6 and a range of 0.4. Neptune has a magnitude of about 8 and a range of 0.2. But Pluto changes from about 12.8 to 15.1, giving a range of 2.3 magnitudes, which means a difference in brightness of 8.5 times.

The range of brightness of each planet is shown in Fig. 7-4 and the data are contained in Table IV.

In Fig. 7-4 the numbers on the left of the main vertical line are magnitudes. A difference of 5 magnitudes equals a ratio of 100 times in brightness. The numbers on the right represent multiples of a unit of brightness which has been taken as that of a star of the sixth magnitude. Uranus has about this magnitude. Therefore, Aldebaran of the first magnitude is 5 magnitudes or 100 times brighter than Uranus. Venus at a magnitude of −4 is 10 magnitudes or 10,000 times brighter than Uranus.

To avoid making the diagram too long, Neptune and Pluto have been placed on separate magnitude scales. The relative brightness is not given for them, but it can be calculated. The difference in magnitude between Venus at its brightest (−4.4) and Pluto at its faintest (+15.1) is 19.5 magnitudes. A difference of 20 magnitudes gives a ratio of 100,000,000. The figure for 19.5 magnitudes is 63,000,000.

Table V gives the ranges in distances of the planets from the earth and the ranges in angular diameters.

TABLE V

	Smallest Distance	Greatest Distance	Greatest Polar Diameter	Smallest Polar Diameter
	(Millions of Miles)			
Mercury	51	135	12".2	4".6
Venus	25	162	64 .5	9 .7
Mars	35	249	25 .1	3 .5
Jupiter	367	600	46 .6	28 .5
Saturn	748	1028	18 .5	13 .5
Uranus	1610	1960		*3"
Neptune	2680	2915		*2"
Pluto	2660	4680		*0".2

Approximate mean values.

Fig. 7-5 shows how much the planets change in apparent size as their distances from the earth vary. The largest and smallest diameters are given for all the planets except Uranus, Neptune, and Pluto, whose diameters are difficult to measure and are somewhat uncertain. A distinction

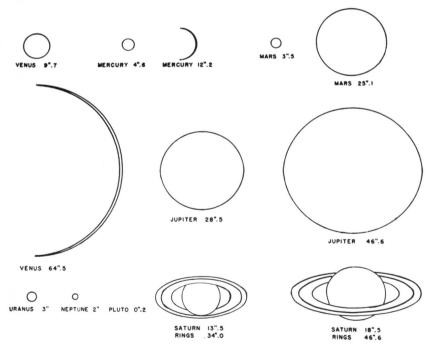

Fig. 7-5. Ranges in apparent sizes of the planets.

has to be made between polar and equatorial diameters, because most of the planets are bulged at the equator. This is called oblateness and is defined as the fraction obtained by dividing the difference between the equatorial and polar diameters by the equatorial.

Saturn has the largest oblateness. The equatorial diameter is 74,200 miles and its polar diameter is 66,400. The difference is 7,800 miles, which is nearly equal to the earth's diameter. The oblateness is about 10 per cent. For Jupiter the diameters are 88,800 and 83,000 miles, giving an oblateness of 6.5 per cent.

The last factor which affects the brightness of a planet is its albedo or reflecting power. It is the ratio of the total amount of sunlight reflected by it in all directions to the amount that falls upon it. In round numbers, the values range from 0.06 for Mercury to 0.75 for Venus. The other three are 0.15 for Mars and 0.50 for Jupiter and Saturn. For comparison, the earth's albedo is about 0.40.

Thus we see how and why the planets change so much in apparent size and brightness. The diagrams may make it a little clearer than has been generally realized how great these changes are.

8

A Star's Daily Path Across the Sky

If a star rises at the east point of the horizon, it will set at the west point, which is directly opposite or 180° from the east point. A person who has not observed the daily path of a star, a planet or the moon across the sky might conclude that if one of these rises in the southeast it will set in the opposite direction, that is, the northwest. However, most of us are familiar with the positions of the sunrise and sunset points, which are not opposite each other, except at the times of the equinoxes.

For example, at Los Angeles on June 21 the sun rises 29° north of the east point and sets 29° north of the west point. Six months later it rises 29° south of the east point and sets 29° south of the west point. The daily path of any celestial object is similar to that of the sun, depending on its distance from the celestial equator (declination) and the observer's distance from the earth's equator (latitude).

Diagrams have been prepared to show the daily path of any celestial object across the sky for the latitudes of 34° and 42° North. Before looking at them, however, we shall define a few terms and illustrate them with the help of Fig. 8-1, which shows how the sun moves across the sky on about May 1 at a latitude of 34° North.

The observer's position is at the lower center of the diagram in the middle of the ellipse which represents a foreshortened view of his horizon. The vertical leads to his zenith, which is a point directly over his head. The half circle extending from the south point of the horizon to the north point and passing through the zenith is the meridian.

The sun is shown at its highest position for the day, when it is on the meridian. Its height or angular distance above the horizon is called its altitude. This ranges from 0° at the horizon to 90° at the zenith. In Fig. 8-1 the sun's altitude is 70°. By subtracting this from 90°, we get its zenith distance of 20°.

The circle from the zenith through the sun at noon reaches the horizon at the south point, which is 180° from the north point. This angular distance measured from the north point toward the east along the horizon to the vertical circle is called azimuth. For example, the azimuth of the east point is 90° and that of the west point is 270°.

The north pole of the sky is directly over the earth's north pole. Its altitude is always equal to the latitude. In Fig. 8-1 it is 34°. The latitude is also equal to the zenith distance of the celestial equator. When the navigator "shoots" the sun at noon, he measures with a sextant the sun's altitude on the meridian. He subtracts this from 90° to get the zenith distance. His almanac gives him the sun's declination, which is its angular distance from the celestial equator. Declination in the sky is just like latitude on the earth. Fig. 8-1 shows how the latitude is equal to the sum of the sun's zenith distance and its declination. In this case the zenith distance is 20° and the declination is 14°, giving a latitude of 34°.

Let us now turn to Fig. 8-2, which shows for the latitude of Los Angeles, 34° N., the daily paths of stars at declinations ranging from −50° to +60°. Each degree of azimuth is shown in the circular band around the outside of the diagram. Numbers from 0 to 350 indicate the azimuth at intervals of 10°. Lines radiating from the center mark the azimuth at intervals of 5°.

Altitude is marked on the diagram at intervals of 10° along the vertical line, which is the celestial meridian running from N, the north point of the horizon, to S, the south point. The zenith is at the center and the concentric circles around it are 2° apart.

A star lying on the celestial equator rises at the east point (azimuth, 90°) and sets at the west point (azimuth, 270°). A star with a declination of +30° rises 37° north of the east point at an azimuth of 53° (90° − 37°). It sets 37° north of the west point at an azimuth of 307° (270° + 37°). A star with a declination of −30° rises 37° south of the east at an azimuth of 127° (90° + 37°). It sets 37° south of the west point at 233° (270° − 37°).

At a latitude of 34° N. a star on the celestial equator crosses the meridian at an altitude of 56° (90° − 34°). A star with a declination of +30° has a

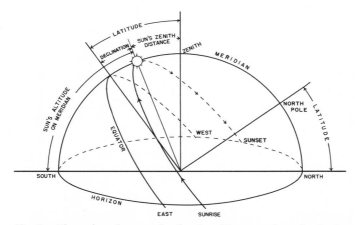

Fig. 8-1. *The sun's path across the sky about May 1 at a latitude of 34° N.*

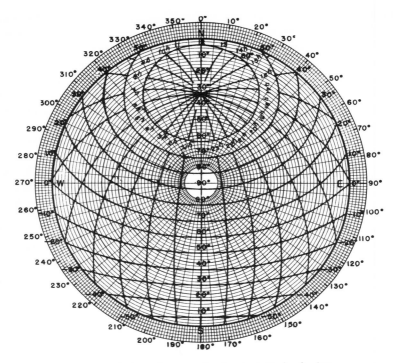

Fig. 8-2. Daily paths across the sky at a latitude of 34° N.

meridian altitude of 86° (56° + 30°) and a star with a declination of −30° crosses the meridian at an altitude of 26° (56° − 30°). The most southerly star which can be observed (neglecting refraction, which is the bending of light by the atmosphere) has a declination of −56°.

Stars having declinations north of +56° are within 34° of the north celestial pole and remain above the horizon all the time at a latitude of 34° N. For example, the daily path of a star at a declination of +60° is completely shown, being 30° from the pole. It crosses the meridian at altitudes of 64° (34° + 30°) and 4° (34° − 30°).

Fig. 8-3 is similar to Fig. 8-2, but it is made for the latitude of 42° and the celestial equator crosses the meridian at an altitude of 48°. The daily paths are similar to those in Fig. 8-2, but the meridian crossing points are 8° farther to the south. Also a star with a given declination rises farther away from the east point and sets farther away from the west point.

The daily path of a star across the sky depends on its declination and the latitude of the observer. The position of the star on that path depends on the right ascension of the star and the local time of the observer. Right ascension is the angular distance from the vernal equinox eastward along the celestial equator to the hour circle of the star. An hour circle is a half circle from pole to pole, like a meridian on the earth. Portions of 24 hour circles are shown in Figs. 8-2 and 8-3. They are measured westward from the meridian and are marked from 1^h to 23^h.

These hour circles are used to indicate local hour angle, which is the angular distance of an hour circle measured westward from the meridian. The local hour angle of a star is equal to the local sidereal time minus the star's right ascension.

Sidereal time is the hour angle of the vernal equinox and it agrees with ordinary time about September 21. It gains 3^m 56^s a day, which accumulates to 2 hours in a month and to a whole day in one year. The gain of sidereal time on civil or ordinary time is given in Table VI, which tabulates the values for every five days. The value for any date can be found by allowing four minutes for each day. The date used should be the local date of the beginning of the night.

In order to find the local sidereal time, it is first necessary to know how much the local civil time differs from the standard time. This depends on the longitude. For example, the longitude of Los Angeles is about 7^h 53^m

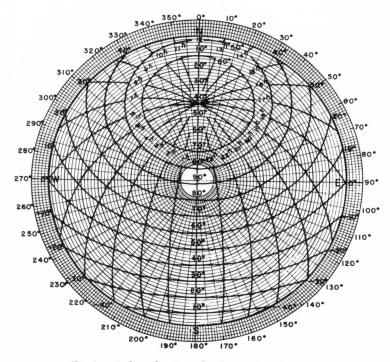

Fig. 8-3. Daily paths across the sky at a latitude of 42° N.

west and the longitude of Pacific Standard Time is 8^h west. Therefore, Los Angeles is 7 minutes east of the standard meridian and its local civil time is 7 minutes ahead of Pacific Standard Time.

Suppose that we wish to find the local sidereal time in Los Angeles on November 16 at 9:15 P.M., PST. We must first express this on a 24-hour basis counted from midnight. Adding 12 hours to the P.M. time, we get $21^h 15^m$ PST. Adding 7 minutes for the longitude of Los Angeles, we get $21^h 22^m$ as the local civil time. From Table VI we find that on November 16 the sidereal time is $3^h 42^m$ ahead of civil time. Adding this amount, we get $24^h 64^m$, or $1^h 04^m$, as the local sidereal time. This is correct within a few minutes, which is close enough for our purpose.

Now that we have the local sidereal time, we subtract from it the right ascension of any celestial object and get its local hour angle. For example, the right ascension of Fomalhaut is $22^h 55^m$ and so its local hour angle is $2^h 09^m$. Its declination is $-30°$. By referring to Fig. 8-2, we find an altitude of $19°$ and an azimuth of $210°$.

Suppose that an observer at this same time and place is trying to find a comet, whose right ascension and declination are known. If he has a suitable star map and if he knows the constellations well, he can plot the comet's position and point his telescope at the approximate location of the comet. Setting circles on the telescope and a sidereal clock would help still more. However, even without these he can find the comet's altitude and azimuth by the method described here. With practice he can learn to estimate the approximate position in the sky of an object whose altitude and azimuth are known. If his latitude lies between 34° N. and 42° N., he can use both diagrams and interpolate between them.

TABLE VI
Gain of Sidereal Time on Civil Time

	Day 5	10	15	20	25	30
January	$7^h 00^m$	$7^h 20^m$	$7^h 40^m$	$7^h 59^m$	$8^h 19^m$	$8^h 39^m$
February	9 02	9 22	9 42	10 02	10 21	—
March	10 53	11 12	11 32	11 52	12 12	12 31
April	12 55	13 15	13 34	13 54	14 14	14 34
May	14 54	15 13	15 33	15 52	16 12	16 32
June	16 55	17 15	17 35	17 55	18 14	18 34
July	18 54	19 13	19 33	19 53	20 12	20 32
August	20 56	21 16	21 35	21 55	22 15	22 35
September	22 58	23 18	23 38	23 57	0 17	0 37
October	0 56	1 16	1 36	1 56	2 15	2 35
November	2 59	3 18	3 38	3 58	4 18	4 37
December	4 57	5 17	5 36	5 56	6 16	6 36

9

The Sun's Daily Path
Across the Sky

We shall first explain the changes in the hours of sunlight and in the sun's daily path across the sky at widely separated latitudes at different times of the year. Then by means of two diagrams for the latitudes of 34° N. and 42° N. we shall see how to find the sun's position with respect to the horizon at any hour of the year.

Fig. 9-1 shows the earth on June 21, with the hours of sunshine ranging from 24 inside the Arctic Circle to none inside the Antarctic Circle. Fig. 9-2 shows the conditions exactly reversed on December 22.

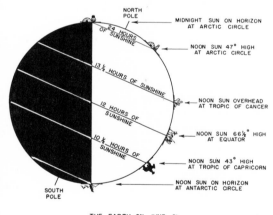

THE EARTH ON JUNE 21

Fig. 9-1.

An observer on the surface of the earth sees only half the celestial sphere at any one time. If he is at either pole, his horizon coincides with the celestial equator, as shown in Fig. 9-3. All the stars north of the celestial equator remain continuously above the horizon at the north pole and all those south of the celestial equator remain continuously above the horizon at the south pole. Their daily paths are parallel to the horizon.

Since the sun is north of the celestial equator half of the time, it remains above the horizon at the north pole for six months from the March equinox to the September equinox. During the other six months it is above the horizon at the south pole.

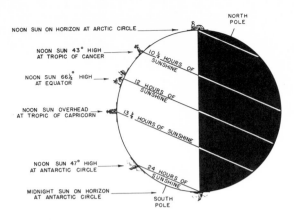

NORTH POLE

NOON SUN ON HORIZON AT ARCTIC CIRCLE

NOON SUN 43° HIGH AT TROPIC OF CANCER

10 ½ HOURS OF SUNSHINE

NOON SUN 66½° HIGH AT EQUATOR

12 HOURS OF SUNSHINE

NOON SUN OVERHEAD AT TROPIC OF CAPRICORN

13 ½ HOURS OF SUNSHINE

NOON SUN 47° HIGH AT ANTARCTIC CIRCLE

24 HOURS OF SUNSHINE

MIDNIGHT SUN ON HORIZON AT ANTARCTIC CIRCLE

SOUTH POLE

THE EARTH ON DECEMBER 22

Fig. 9-2.

In Fig. 9-4 the sky appears as seen from the equator. In these diagrams the zenith is always at the top, because each person feels that he is on top of the world, regardless of his position. The celestial equator passes through this observer's zenith and all the stars rise and set vertically to the horizon. The daily path of each one is cut in half by the horizon. This is true of the sun, which is above the horizon 12 hours every day of the year.

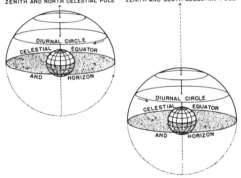

ZENITH AND NORTH CELESTIAL POLE   ZENITH AND SOUTH CELESTIAL POLE

DIURNAL CIRCLE
CELESTIAL   EQUATOR
AND   HORIZON

DIURNAL CIRCLE
CELESTIAL   EQUATOR
AND   HORIZON

Fig. 9-3. The sky as seen from the earth's two poles, where the stars do not rise or set.

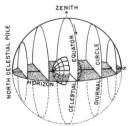

ZENITH

NORTH CELESTIAL POLE

EQUATOR

DIURNAL CIRCLE

HORIZON

CELESTIAL

Fig. 9-4. The sky as seen from the equator, where all the stars rise and set.

This is brought out in Fig. 9-5, which shows the sun's daily paths across the sky at the equator on three different dates. Since it is 23½° south of the celestial equator on December 21, it is that same distance south of

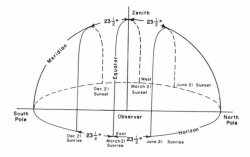

Fig. 9-5. *The sun's daily paths across the sky at the equator on the 21st of December, March and June.*

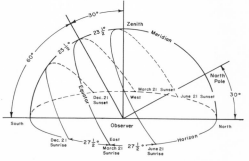

Fig. 9-6. *The sun's daily paths across the sky at a latitude of 30° North of the 21st of December, March and June.*

east at sunrise, south of the zenith at noon, and south of west at sunset. On June 21 it is 23½° north of these points at the corresponding times. On March 21 (and also on September 22) the sun rises in the east, passes through the zenith, and sets in the west.

As we move northward from the equator to a latitude of 30° North, we move our zenith 30° north of the celestial equator and we tip our north horizon 30° below the north celestial pole. Fig. 9-6 shows the sun's daily paths at the solstices and the equinoxes as seen from the latitude of 30° North. On March 21 the sun rises in the east and sets in the west, crossing the meridian 30° south of the zenith. Since the sun's paths are not perpendicular to the horizon, the sunrise and sunset points on June 21 and December 21 are more than 23½° from their respective east and west points, the distance being 27½°.

Although the sun on June 21 rises 27½° north of east and sets 27½° north of west, it crosses the meridian 6½° south of the zenith. This is found by subtracting 23½° from the latitude of 30°. On December 21 the noon sun is 47° (twice 23½°) lower than on June 21.

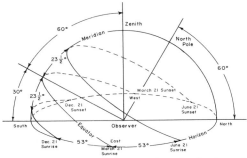

Fig. 9-7. The sun's daily paths across the sky at a latitude of 60° North on the 21st of December, March and June.

Moving to the latitude of 60° North in Fig. 9-7, we find the sun on June 21 rising 53° north of east and setting 53° north of west. Also in December it rises 53° south of east and sets 53° south of west. The zenith is 60° north of the celestial equator, which crosses the meridian 30° above the south point of the horizon. Since the sun is 23½° south of the equator on December 21, it gets only 6½° high at noon on that date.

Another way of looking at the sun's path is shown in the next three diagrams, where the zenith is at the center of a circle representing the horizon. Hour divisions are marked along the sun's paths. Fig. 9-8 is for the equator, where the sun rises at about 6 A.M. and sets at about 6 P.M. every day of the year.

At the latitude of 30° North shown in Fig. 9-9, the sun is up 14 hours on June 21, rising at 5 A.M. and setting at 7 P.M. On December 21 it is up 10 hours, rising at 7 A.M. and setting at 5 P.M.

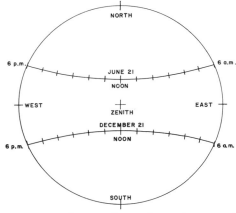

Fig. 9-8. In this and the next two diagrams the zenith is at the center of a circle representing the horizon. This shows the sun's daily paths at the equator on June 21 and December 21.

100

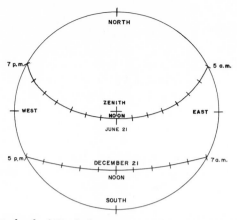

Fig. 9-9. At a latitude of 30° North the sun is up 14 hours on June 21 and 10 hours on December 21.

Fig. 9-10 brings out the great seasonal changes in the sun's path at high latitudes. At 60° North on June 21 the sun rises at 2:30 A.M. and sets at 9:30 P.M. It gets only 6½° below the horizon at midnight, when the sky is still fairly bright, since twilight lasts until the sun is 18° below the horizon. The sun rises closer to the north point than the east point, and sets closer to the north point than the west point. On December 21 the sun is up only 6 hours, is only 6½° high at noon, and is never more than 37° away from the south point.

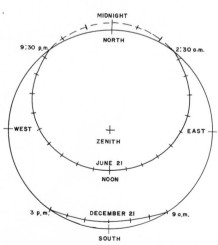

Fig. 9-10. At a latitude of 60° North the sun on June 21 rises closer to the north point than the east point and sets closer to the north point than the west point. On December 21 the situation is the same with respect to the south point.

Thus we see that the statement, "The sun rises in the east and sets in the west," is strictly true only at the times of the equinoxes, which are about March 21 and September 22. Visitors to such places as Alaska can get their directions quite mixed up, if they depend on the sun and do not realize how much its rising and setting positions change during the year.

Fig. 9-11 shows the sun's daily path across the sky on or about the 21st of each month at the latitude of Los Angeles, 34° N. Fig. 9-12 is a similar diagram for the latitude of 42° N. This can be used for such cities as New York, Boston, Philadelphia, Cleveland, Detroit, and Chicago. In fact, from these two diagrams, one can determine the approximate position of the sun with respect to the horizon of most places in the United States at any hour of the year.

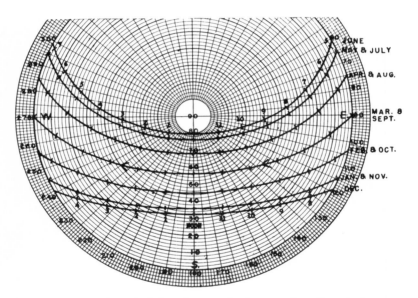

Fig. 9-11. The sun's daily path across the sky on or about the 21st of each month at a latitude of 34° N.

The sun's position with reference to the horizon is expressed by altitude and azimuth. Altitude is the angular distance above the horizon measured perpendicular to the horizon. It has a maximum value of 90° at the zenith, which is the point overhead. It is marked on the diagram at intervals of 10° along the vertical line in the center. That line represents the celestial meridian, which the sun crosses at noon. An altitude can be read at any time of the day by means of concentric circles which are 2° apart.

Azimuth is the angular distance measured along the horizon from the north point in a clockwise direction. North is 0°, east is 90°, south is 180°, and west is 270°. Each degree of azimuth is shown in the circular band around the outside of the diagram, and numbers from 60 to 300 indicate the azimuth at intervals of 10°. Lines radiating from the center mark the azimuth at intervals of 5°.

The sun's daily path across the sky on or about the 21st day of each month is indicated by means of seven curved lines. The upper one is for June and the lower one is for December. Each of the other five is for two months. For instance, the path on March 21 is the same as on September 23.

Each path is divided into hours. Numbers along the upper and lower paths show the hours which would be indicated by a sundial. This is known as local apparent sun time. Standard time will differ from this, depending on the equation of time and the longitude. However, this uncertainty is not important for our purpose, which is to show the general course of the sun across the sky and not its exact position at any particular instant of time.

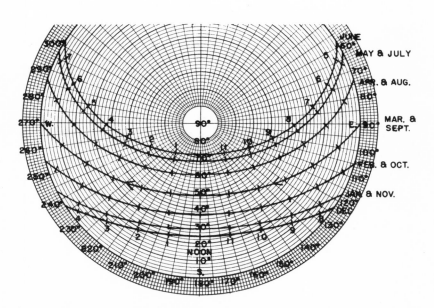

Fig. 9-12. The sun's daily path across the sky on or about the 21st of each month at a latitude of 42° N.

It is interesting to see how much the sunrise and sunset points move during the year. The azimuth of the extreme positions are as follows:

	Sunrise	Sunset
June 21	61°	299°
Dec. 21	119°	241°
Difference	58°	58°

In other words, the sun rises 29° south of east and sets 29° south of west on December 21. This is for a latitude of 34° N. The arc of the horizon between the east point and the sunrise point is called amplitude. On June 21 it is 23½° at the equator, and increases to 90° at the Arctic Circle, where the sun is up for 24 hours on that day. The value at a latitude of 42° N. is 32½°.

On March 21 and September 23 the sun is on the celestial equator, which intersects the celestial meridian at a distance from the zenith equal to the latitude. At a latitude of 34° N. on these dates the noon sun is 34° south of the zenith. Its altitude is 56°, which is found by subtracting 34° from 90°.

On June 21 the sun is 23½° north of the celestial equator and its maximum altitude at noon is 79½°, which is the sum of 56° and 23½°. On December 21 the sun is 23½° south of the celestial equator and its noon altitude is 32½°, which is the difference between 56° and 23½°. Thus the sun's meridian altitude varies by 47°. This range is twice 23½° and is the same for all latitudes.

The approximate duration of sunlight can be estimated from the diagram. The upper curve for June 21 shows that the sun rises at about 4:45 A.M. and sets at about 7:15 P.M., giving a duration of 14½ hours. On May 21 and July 21 the sun is up for 14 hours. The number for March and September is 12 hours. There are nearly 10 hours of sunshine on the shortest day.

It is interesting to notice that on June 21 the sun is north of the east-west line for a longer time than it is south of it. It is hoped that these diagrams will not only be of general interest but will also be useful to the architect who wants to know how the sun will shine on the windows and other parts of a building at all times of the year.

10
Sun Time

Timekeeping is based upon the period in which the earth makes a rotation on its axis. We keep track of the earth's eastward turning by observing the apparent westward motion of the heavens which it causes. One rotation is called a day, but there are several different kinds of day, depending on what celestial object is used as a time reckoner.

The true period of the earth's rotation is called a sidereal day, meaning a day measured with respect to the stars. A solar day is not equal to a sidereal day, because the stars appear as fixed points in space and the sun appears to move eastward with respect to the stars about one degree per day. This apparent motion is caused by the earth's annual revolution around the sun.

Since the earth is turning on its axis to the east and is also revolving around the sun in the same direction, it makes more than a complete turn during one solar day. The extra amount is about one degree, since there are 365 days in a year and 360° in a circle. If the sun's apparent eastward progress against the background of stars were uniform, all solar days would be equal. However, this is not so, and hence the sun in the sky can not be used as a reliable timekeeper. There are two reasons for this irregularity.

The first reason results from what are known as Kepler's laws. There are three of them, but only the first two concern us here. The first law is that the planets move around the sun in ellipses, having the sun in a common focus. The second law is that each planet revolves in such a way that the imaginary line joining it to the sun sweeps over equal areas in equal intervals of time.

Fig. 10-1 illustrates these laws. The shape of the earth's elliptical orbit has been greatly exaggerated in order to make the principles clear. If the orbit were drawn correctly to scale, it would look just like a circle on such a small diagram. On about January 2 the earth is at perihelion, its nearest position to the sun. The distance is then 91,500,000 miles. On about July 4 the earth is at aphelion, its most distant point from the sun. The distance is then 94,500,000 miles. Thus the mean distance is 93,000,000 miles.

For the sake of clarity, the distance covered by the earth in one day has

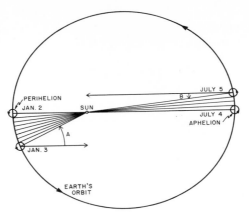

Fig. 10-1. Kepler's law of equal areas.

also been made too large. The diagram shows in an exaggerated way that the earth moves faster in its orbit when nearest the sun that when farthest away. The area swept out by the line joining the earth to the sun from January 2 to January 3 is equal to the area swept out by a similar line from July 4 to July 5. Since the January earth-sun line is shorter than the July line, the earth moves faster in January than in July, in order for the two areas to be equal.

The angle A shows how much longer the solar day is than the sidereal day in January. The long horizontal arrow at January 3 points in the direction in which an observer was looking at noon on January 2. It will not be noon on January 3 for that observer until the earth has turned through the extra angle A. Similarly the angle B shows how much longer the solar day is than the sidereal day in July. Since angle A is larger than angle B, the solar day in January is longer than the solar day in July, taking into consideration this one cause alone.

The second reason for the sun's irregular eastward motion can be explained with the aid of Figs. 10-2 and 10-3. They show two portions of the ecliptic, which is the sun's apparent annual path among the stars. The horizontal line near the bottom is the celestial equator, which runs in an east-west direction. The ecliptic is inclined to the equator at an angle of 23½°. The intersection of these two lines is shown in Fig. 10-3 and is the vernal equinox. That is the point where the sun appears on March 21.

Corresponding to longitude on the earth is a term known as right ascension in the sky. It is measured from the vernal equinox eastward along the celestial equator. It is expressed in hours, each hour being equal to 15°. The hours of right ascension are marked along the equator and increase to the left, which is to the east on star maps. The dashed lines represent hour circles, which come together at the celestial poles in the same way that meridians converge at the poles of the earth.

The point where the ecliptic crosses the hour circle at 6 hours is the summer solstice, which the sun reaches on June 21. That point is 23½° north of the celestial equator. The hour circles are closer together along that part of the ecliptic than they are along the equator. That is shown by the heavy portion of the ecliptic which is 30° long. It is seen to extend from the hour circle at 4 hours to a short distance beyond the hour circle at 6 hours. Also the sun's path in June is nearly parallel to the equator, and should be compared with the path in March.

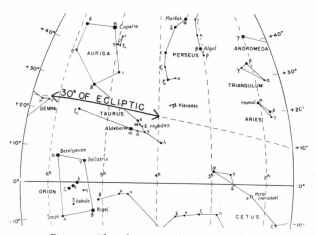

Fig. 10-2. *The ecliptic near the summer solstice.*

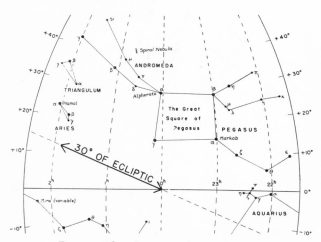

Fig. 10-3. *The ecliptic near the vernal equinox.*

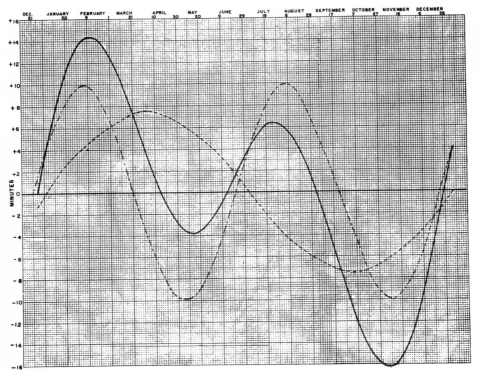

Fig. 10-4. The equation of time.

Fig. 10-3 shows 30° marked along the ecliptic, starting at 0 hours, but falling short of the hour circle at 2 hours. The reason for this is that the direction in which the sun is moving is considerably to the north as well as to the east. The sun does not make as rapid progress eastward, because it is, in effect, wasting part of its motion by going northward.

Thus we see that even if the sun's motion along the ecliptic were uniform, its eastward progress would not be regular. At the times of the equinoxes (March and September), the sun is moving eastward more slowly than the average. At the times of the solstices (June and December), it is moving eastward more rapidly than the average.

The effects of the eccentricity of the earth's orbit and of the inclination of the ecliptic to the celestial equator upon the length of the solar day are small. The longest day in the year (December 23) is only about 51 seconds longer than the shortest day (September 17). It should be noted that the word "day" here means the interval from one noon to the next and does not mean the length of time the sun is above the horizon.

Although the variation in the length of a true solar day is not large, the difference accumulates day after day and at times reaches about a quarter of an hour. Since the sun is a poor timekeeper, a fictitious sun has been invented. It is called the mean sun and may be thought of as an imaginary point moving eastward uniformly along the celestial equator at the average rate of the true or apparent sun. It will be noted that it is customary to call the real sun in the sky the apparent sun.

The length of the mean solar day is the average of the lengths of all the apparent solar days in a year. The mean solar day is divided into 24 mean solar hours, and these are the hours kept by our watches. Mean solar time is the time in ordinary use all over the world.

The difference between mean solar time and apparent solar time is called the equation of time.

Mean time − apparent time = equation of time.

From this we get:

Mean time = apparent time + equation of time.

The values of the equation of time throughout the year are plotted in the diagram (Fig. 10-4) containing three curves. The minutes are marked vertically at the left side, plus above the zero line and minus below it. The curve which is above the line from January 2 to July 4 and below the line the other half of the year represents the equation due to the eccentricity of the earth's orbit. Considering only the varying speed of the earth around the sun and hence of the sun along the ecliptic, we can see that if

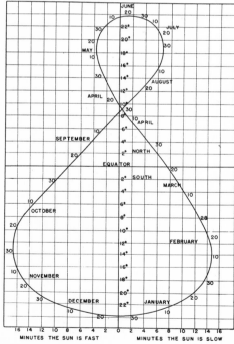

Fig. 10-5. The analemma. The vertical scale shows how many degrees the sun is north or south of the equator. The horizontal scale gives the difference between local clock time and sun time.

the mean and apparent suns coincide on January 2 at perihelion, the apparent sun will be east of the mean sun for the first six months of the year. The apparent sun is moving eastward at its greatest rate on January 2 and will come to the meridian later and later each day for about three months. As the apparent sun slows down, the mean sun gradually catches up to it and the two coincide at aphelion on about July 4, when the earth is moving most slowly.

During the second half of the year the apparent sun is behind the mean sun, that is, to the west of it. Therefore, the daily turning of the earth makes it come to the meridian early. The daily differences sum up to a maximum difference of nearly +8 minutes about the first of April and of nearly −8 minutes about the first of October.

Considering now only the sun's irregularity due to the inclination of the ecliptic to the celestial equator, we look at the curve which crosses the zero line at December 21, March 21, June 21, and September 23. If the mean and apparent suns coincided at the vernal equinox on March 21, one moving uniformly along the equator and the other along the ecliptic, they would be together at the autumnal equinox on September 23. That is because the equinoxes are 180° apart, measured along both the equator and the ecliptic. The solstices are exactly halfway between the equinoxes, and so the mean and apparent suns would be on the same hour circle on those dates, June 21 and December 21.

The heavy-line curve represents the combined effect of the two causes. The vertical distance from the zero line of any point on this curve is equal to the algebraic sum of the vertical distances of corresponding points on the other two curves. Thus in the middle of February the heavy curve has a large positive value, resulting from the fact that the two component curves are both well above the zero line at that time. Around the first of November both these curves are well below the line and they produce a negative value of more than 16 minutes. The equation of time becomes zero four times yearly. The dates vary slightly from year to year, but are about April 15, June 15, September 1, and December 25.

If we were to fold the diagram along a vertical line passing through June 21 and were then to look through the paper toward the light, we would see a figure "8", lying on its side. Turning it around so that the small loop is at the top, we would see the resemblance between this and the analemma shown in the next diagram.

The analemma (Fig. 10-5) shows not only how many minutes the sun is fast or slow, but also how far north or south of the equator the sun is on any date. Thus it will be seen that the sun is 23½° north of the equator on June 21, 23½° south of it on December 21, and on the equator on March 21 and September 23. The analemma is commonly marked on terrestrial globes as a long, slim figure. Here is has been broadened somewhat by making the scale for minutes four times larger. This makes it easier to read. One minute of time has been represented by the same space as one degree. Actually the earth rotates through an angle of one degree in four minutes of time.

The equation of time has an interesting effect upon the mean time of sunrise and sunset near the winter solstice. The analemma shows that the sun is about 12 minutes fast on December 1 and about 14 minutes slow at the end of January. Thus the sun loses 26 minutes in two months, which is at the rate of nearly half a minute a day. Its apparent eastward motion is greater than that of the mean sun, and it comes to the meridian later and later each day, as measured by a clock. On about December 25 the equation of time is zero. When it is noon by the clock on that day, it is also noon by the sun. The next day when it is noon by the clock, it will be about 30 seconds before noon by the sun. Since the lengths of the days are not increasing much at this time of the year, the interval from sunrise till mean solar noon will decrease nearly 30 seconds. That will make the clock time of sunrise a little later each day, even though the interval from sunrise to sunset is increasing. The interval from noon by the clock till sunset will increase by a little more than 30 seconds each day at this time of the year.

This may be summed up by saying that while the mornings are decreasing in length, the afternoons and the whole periods from sunrise to sunset are increasing. The earliest sunsets occur about two weeks before the winter solstice. The latest sunrises occur about two weeks after the winter solstice.

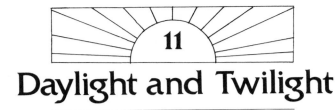

Daylight and Twilight

At the equinoxes in March and September the night is equal in length to the day all over the world. This statement is only approximately true, for two reasons. If the sun were a point source of light like a star and if the earth had no atmosphere, then there would be exactly 12 hours of sunshine at all latitudes on March 21 and September 23, and at the equator every day.

Since the sun is not a point, we get a little extra sunshine. Sunrise and sunset are the times at which the upper edge of the sun's disk is seen, and not when the center of the sun's disk appears. The sun's radius is 16'. Also the earth's atmosphere refracts or bends the sun's light, raising the apparent direction of the sun at the horizon by about 34'. Adding these two angles, we get 50', which is 5/6 of a degree. Since the earth turns through one degree in four minutes, we get about 3⅓ extra minutes of sunshine at sunrise and the same amount at sunset, making a total of nearly 7 minutes.

Thus the interval from sunrise to sunset at the equator is 12 hours and 7 minutes every day in the year. The sun rises at right angles to the horizon at the equator, but it moves slantingly at other latitudes, thus slightly increasing the duration of sunlight. For example, on March 21, when there are 12 hours and 7 minutes of sunshine at the equator, we find 12 hours and 9 minutes at Los Angeles (34°N.) and 12 hours and 20 minutes at Fairbanks, Alaska (65°N.).

Because of the extra seven minutes, we would expect the sun to rise at the equator every day just before $5^h 57^m$ and to set just after $18^h 03^m$ (6:03 P.M.). However, the sun is not a reliable timekeeper and our watches can not follow its irregular motion. In January the earth is 3,000,000 miles nearer the sun than in July, and it travels a little faster. This makes the sun's apparent eastward motion with respect to the stars a little greater in January than in July.

A second reason for the irregularity is that the earth's equator is inclined to its orbit. The sun's apparent annual motion on the celestial sphere is parallel to the equator at the solstices. At those times it makes more rapid progress to the east than when its motion is at an angle to the equator as in March and September. Only eastward motion affects the length of the day.

Because of the sun's irregularity, an imaginary sun has been invented. It is a smooth-running timekeeper, so that its day has the same length throughout the year, the average of all apparent solar days. The average sun is called the "mean" sun, and the time which it keeps is "mean" solar time, used in ordinary life. The difference between apparent solar time and mean solar time is called the equation of time. A more detailed description of this matter is given in the chapter entitled "Sun Time."

If we define the equation of time as mean time minus apparent time, we find that its value ranges from plus 14 minutes and 20 seconds on February 12 to minus 16 minutes and 24 seconds on November 4. If we apply these corrections to the previously calculated times of sunrise ($5^h 57^m$) and of sunset ($18^h 03^m$), we get the following times for the equator on these two dates:

	Sunrise	Sunset
February 12	$6^h 11^m$	$18^h 18^m$
November 4	$5^h 40^m$	$17^h 47^m$

The shifting of these times throughout the year is shown in Fig. 11-1. The upper part gives the times of sunrise and sunset on the 21st day of each month from December to June, and the lower part covers from June to December. These are for the northern hemisphere only. Latitude is marked at both sides and time runs from left to right across the middle. Each of the little squares represents one degree of latitude vertically and six minutes of time horizontally. On this scale it is not possible to read the times to the nearest minute, but they should be correct within about three minutes. Also the pen sometimes may have slipped a minute or two.

As an example, let us find the times for latitude 40°N. on December 21. The left half of the curve for that date crosses the 40° line at the third division past 7^h. Therefore, sunrise is at $7^h 18^m$. The right half of the curve intersects the 40° line in the seventh division beyond 16^h. It is closer to the sixth line (36^m) than the seventh line (42^m). The correct time of sunset is $16^h 38^m$ (4:38 P.M.). The duration of daylight is 9 hours and 20 minutes. The corresponding figures for June 21 are $4^h 31^m$ for sunrise, $19^h 32^m$ for sunset, and 15 hours and one minute for duration of daylight.

As we follow the June 21 curves to higher latitudes, we find the sun rising earlier and setting later. The curves hit the midnight line at a latitude of about 65¾°. The Arctic Circle is 66½°, the difference being due to refraction and the radius of the sun, as explained earlier. At the latitude of 65¾° N. the sun is up for 24 hours on June 21. As we go farther north, the

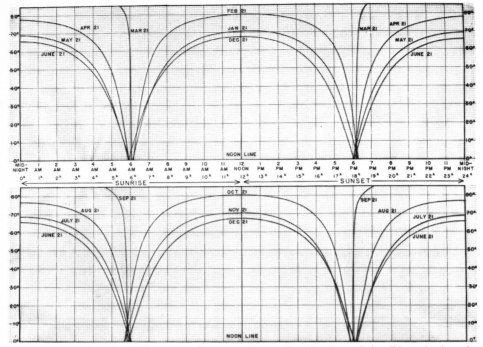

Fig. 11-1. Times of sunrise and sunset on the 21st day of each month for all latitudes from the equator to 85° N.

number of hours of continuous daylight gradually increases from 24 hours to a week, then to a month, and so on until the continuous daylight lasts six months at the north pole.

The December 21 curve crosses the noon line at a latitude of about 67¼° N., which is ¾° north of the Arctic Circle. This means that the sun is below the horizon for 24 hours on that date at that latitude. As we go farther north, the number of hours of continuous lack of daylight gradually increases to a maximum of six months at the north pole. We call it a lack of daylight rather than darkness, because there is considerable twilight at these high latitudes. At the north pole there is about six weeks of it after the sun sets and also before it rises.

If there were no refraction and if the sun were a point, the number of hours of daylight a place would have on June 21 would be the same as the number of hours without daylight on December 21. For example, at a latitude of 49° N. there would be 16 hours of daylight on June 21 and 16 hours without daylight on December 21. Because of refraction and the sun's disk, the actual duration of daylight is 14 minutes more than 16 hours on June 21 and 14 minutes more than 8 hours on December 21.

Without refraction and without the sun's being a disk, the total number of hours of daylight which any place would have during the year would equal the total number of hours without daylight. Actually the daylight hours are somewhat greater. For example, at the equator each day the sun is up for about 14 minutes more than it is down. This adds up to about 85 hours for the whole year. The excess is greater for other latitudes.

The times of sunrise and sunset on the chart are expressed in terms of local civil time. To find the reading of your watch, which keeps standard time, a correction must be applied for longitude. For example, since Los Angeles is seven minutes east of the standard meridian, we must subtract seven minutes from its local civil time to get Pacific Standard Time. Similarly, we add ten minutes to the local time of San Francisco to get standard time, because that city is ten minutes west of the 120th meridian. To get daylight saving time, add one hour to standard time.

In order to find the times of sunrise and sunset for any date other than the 21st, we interpolate. For example, let us determine the time of sunrise on August 1 at a latitude of 60° N. The curve for July 21 crosses the 60° line in the middle of the third division between 3^h and 4^h. Since each division is 6 minutes, that time is $3^h 15^m$. The curve for August 21 crosses the 60° line almost exactly half way between 4^h and 5^h. Therefore, we shall call it $4^h 30^m$. The difference between $4^h 30^m$ and $3^h 15^m$ is $1^h 15^m$ or 75^m.

The interval from July 21 to August 1 is 11 days, which is about a third of a month. One third of 75 minutes is 25 minutes. Adding that to $3^h 15^m$, we get $3^h 40^m$, the local civil time of sunrise at 60° N. on August 1.

The times plotted in Fig. 11-1 are taken from a supplement to the *American Ephemeris*, 1946, entitled "Tables of Sunrise, Sunset and Twilight." This publication is issued by the Nautical Almanac Office of the United States Naval Observatory.

Coming now to the matter of twilight, we shall quote from the above publication which defines three kinds of twilight as follows:

"The duration of civil twilight is the interval in the evening from sunset

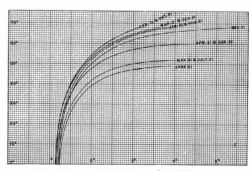

Fig. 11-2. Duration of twilight.

Fig. 11-3. Twilight at equator. (left)
Fig. 11-4. Twilight at 31° N. (right)

until the time when the center of the sun is 6° below the horizon; or the corresponding interval in the morning between sunrise and the time at which the sun was still 6° below the horizon. Civil twilight is intended to cover the somewhat indefinite periods after sunset and before sunrise during which the natural illumination usually remains sufficient for ordinary outdoor operations to be carried on; but actually the illumination during the interval when the sun is less than 6° below the horizon varies greatly according to weather conditions, especially cloudiness and haze, and local surroundings.

"The durations of nautical and astronomical twilight are, respectively, the intervals between sunrise or sunset and the times at which the center of the sun is 12° and 18° below the horizon. The limits of astronomical twilight are the times at which complete darkness (aside from moonlight or starlight) begins in the evening and ends in the morning. Nautical twilight represents an intermediate stage of illumination."

The curves in Fig. 11-2 show the duration of astronomical twilight on the 21st day of each month from the equator to the Arctic Circle. Each of the little squares represents one degree of latitude vertically and three minutes of time horizontally.

From the diagram it is obvious that the duration of twilight is shortest at the equator and increases with increasing distance from the equator. This does not hold true all the way to the pole, because there are intervals of time when there is no twilight at all in the very high latitudes.

The curve for June 21 ends at the latitude of 49°, because that marks the beginning of the zone of continuous twilight between sunset and sunrise on that date. This zone extends to 66°, where the zone of continuous daylight begins. Similarly the curve for May 21 and July 21 ends at 52° and the one for April 21 and August 21 ends at 60°. The other curves could be extended farther, but have been cut off near the Arctic Circle.

The shortest duration of astronomical twilight occurs at the equator at the times of the equinoxes. Then the sun sets at right angles to the horizon and reaches a distance of 18° below the horizon in the shortest possible time. Because of refraction·and the sun's radius, the distance which the sun travels from sunset to the end of twilight is only about 17¼°. It

116

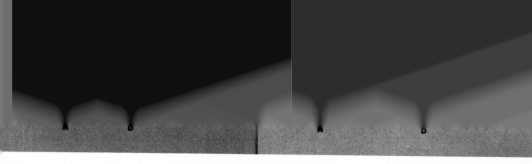

Fig. 11-5. Twilight at 49° N. (left)
Fig. 11-6. Twilight at 68° N. (right)

moves 15° in one hour and 1° in four minutes. Therefore, the shortest duration of twilight is one hour and nine minutes.

One might expect twilight at the equator to have the same length every day in the year. However, Fig. 11-2 shows a range from $1^h\,09^m$ on March 21 and September 21 to $1^h\,15^m$ on June 21 and December 21. On the last two dates the sun is at its maximum distance of 23½° away from the equator, north of it in June and south of it in December. The situation is illustrated in Fig. 11-3.

The white ball represents the celestial sphere. The earth is at the center of this imaginary sphere, to which the celestial bodies seem to be attached. As the earth turns eastward, the celestial sphere seems to turn westward. This is downward in our picture, since we are looking at the west point of the horizon marked W.

The north celestial pole is at the north point of the horizon on the left and the south celestial pole is at the south point of the horizon on the right. Connecting these poles are the hour circles.

The circle passing through W and M is the celestial equator, which is perpendicular to the wide horizontal ring representing the horizon. Since the sun is on the celestial equator at the times of the equinoxes, this circle represents the sun's daily path on those dates. The circle above J is 23½° north of the celestial equator and it shows the sun's daily path on June 21. Similarly the circle above D is 23½° south of the celestial equator and it shows the sun's daily path on December 21.

The horizontal line passing through J, M, and D is 18° below the horizon and marks the ending of twilight. The duration of twilight on March 21 is represented by the vertical line WM below the horizon. Similarly the duration for June 21 is shown by NJ and that for December 21 by SD.

The hour circle between the horizon and the line marking the ending of twilight indicates the positions of celestial objects which are one hour below the horizon. It is obvious that one hour after sunset the sun is farther below the horizon on March 21 than on June 21 and December 21. The distance between two adjacent hour circles is greatest along the celestial equator. Therefore, the duration of twilight at the earth's equator is shortest in March and September and longest in June and December.

The reason for the increase in duration of twilight with the increase in distance from the equator can be seen in Fig. 11-4, which is for the latitude of 31°. This latitude has been chosen because it is where the duration of sunlight is four hours longer on June 21 than on December 21. Instead of going down at right angles to the horizon, as it does at the equator, the sun follows a slanting course and takes a longer time to reach a distance of 18° below the horizon.

The duration of twilight at 31° is shortest in March and September, but the values for June and December are not equal, as they are at the equator. A comparison of the lines NJ (the sun's June path) and SD (the sun's December path) shows that twilight lasts longer in June.

This is brought out more strikingly in Fig. 11-5, where the globe is set for 49° and daylight on June 21 is eight hours longer than on December 21. Here the twilight lasts all night on June 21, as is shown by the fact that J, the sun's position at midnight is less than 18° below the horizon.

In Fig. 11-6 the globe is set for 68°, close to the Arctic Circle. The lowest position of the sun on June 21 is at N, the north point of the horizon, and so there is continuous daylight on that date. The highest position of the sun on December 21 is at S, the south point of the horizon, and so there is no daylight on that date. The long twilight during most of the year at this latitude is illustrated by the length of the lines, WM and SD.

Twilight is caused by the scattering and reflection of sunlight by the earth's atmosphere. When the sun is 18° below the horizon and twilight ends, the sun's rays pass 50 miles above the earth's surface. The atmosphere above this level reflects no perceptible sunlight. However, the atmosphere extends to more than ten times that height, as revealed by measurements of the aurora. If the earth had no atmosphere, the setting of the sun would bring immediate darkness.

The Phases of the Moon

Since the sun's rays come from one direction, they can light up only one half of a sphere at one time. As the earth turns, we get day and night. One half of the moon is in sunlight and one half is in darkness. The phases represent the varying amounts of the moon's sunlit hemisphere which are turned toward the earth as the moon revolves around the earth.

In Fig. 12-1 the sunlight is coming from the right. The moon is new when it passes the sun. The dark hemisphere is turned completely toward the earth, and we can not see the moon at this phase. We can say that new moon is "no moon."

Since the moon's orbit is inclined at an angle of about five degrees to the earth's orbit, the new moon usually passes a little above or below the sun. However, at least twice a year it goes in front of the sun, causing a solar eclipse.

When the moon is in the crescent phase, we can often see the rest of the moon dimly lighted. This has been called "the old moon in the new moon's arms," because the bright crescent seems to be wrapped around the fainter part. (See Fig. 12-2.)

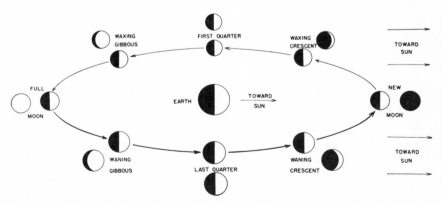

Fig. 12-1. The phases of the moon. The moon is shown in eight different positions in its orbit, one half of the moon being in sunlight and one half in darkness. The outer figures show the phases as seen from the earth. These phases represent the varying amounts of the moon's sunlit hemisphere which are turned toward the earth as the moon revolves around it.

The crescent is receiving direct light from the sun, but the rest of the moon's disk is made visible by sunlight reflected from the earth. As observed from the moon, the earth would appear to go through phases. When we say that the moon is new, an observer on the moon would say that the earth is full. Earthshine on the moon is best seen when the moon is a thin crescent, because the earth is then nearly full in the lunar sky.

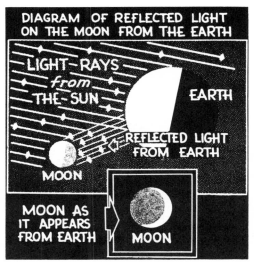

Fig. 12-2.

Earthshine on the moon is much brighter than moonlight on the earth for two reasons. First, the earth's diameter is about 3⅔ that of the moon and its reflecting surface is over 13 times as great, since surfaces vary as the squares of their diameters. Second, on account of the earth's atmosphere and clouds, it is about five times a better reflector than the moon's bare rock surface. The earth must give about 65 times as much light to the moon as the moon gives to the earth.

It takes the moon about seven days to go one quarter of the way around its orbit. The phase of the moon at this position is first quarter. The lighted part of the moon appears as half a circle. The terminator, or boundary between day and night on the moon, appears as a straight line. The most striking views are obtainable near this phase and near last quarter, when the lunar mountains near the terminator cast long dark shadows, which give a fine effect of contrast with the bright parts.

The moon is in the gibbous phase between first quarter and full moon and between full moon and last quarter. The moon is said to be waxing between new moon and full moon, and it is waning from full moon to new moon.

Because of the inclination of the moon's orbit to the earth's orbit, the full moon is usually not exactly opposite the sun, passing a little above or below the earth's shadow. When the full moon goes into that shadow, the resulting lunar eclipse is visible from all of the night side of the earth.

Although the visible lighted part of the moon is constantly changing shape, the same hemisphere of the moon (except for small oscillations) is always turned toward the earth. It is commonly believed that the moon does not rotate on its axis, but if that were so, we would be able to see all around it. It rotates on its axis at the same average rate that it revolves around the earth.

To demonstrate this motion, stand in the center of a room and imagine that you represent the earth. Have another person take the part of the moon and stand a few feet away with his left side toward you. As he walks around you in a circle, he keeps his left side always toward you. You never see his right side. Yet he has faced in all directions and has turned his body completely around. To show what would happen if the moon did not turn on its axis, have your friend walk around you and face the same wall. You see first his left side, then the back of his head, then his right side, and finally you get a direct view of his face.

The moon's period of revolution around the earth from one new moon to the next is about 29½ days, which is about one day less than the average length of a calendar month. This means that the date of any phase of the moon occurs an average of one day earlier from one month to the next. This period of 29½ days is called the synodic month.

The moon's true period of revolution around the earth is the average time between two successive passages in front of the same star. It is called the sidereal month and its average length is 27⅓ days. Since the sun appears to move eastward among the stars nearly 30° during a sidereal month, the moon must travel for about two days more to overtake it.

The moon's eastward motion is 13° per day and the sun's is 1° per day. Therefore, the moon moves eastward 12° each day with respect to the sun. Since the earth turns on its axis at the rate of 1° in 4 minutes, the moon crosses the meridian about 50 minutes later each day. This excess over 24 hours ranges from 38 to 66 minutes. This is due mainly to the changing speed of the moon in its elliptical orbit and the inclination of its path to the celestial equator.

The average delay in the moon's daily rising and setting is also 50 minutes, but this quantity is much more variable. It depends on the latitude and the moon's position in its path. When the moon is near the vernal equinox, its path there makes the smallest angle with the eastern horizon and the moon is moving rapidly northward. This makes the delay in its rising smaller than average.

This becomes most noticeable near the phase of full moon, when the moon rises in the early evening. If the full moon is near the vernal equinox, the sun must be near the autumnal equinox. The full moon occurring nearest September 23 is called the harvest moon. For several evenings the moon rises only a little later each night, so that there is full moonlight in the early evening for an unusual number of days.

In 1975 the moon was full on September 20 and its delay in rising from the previous day was 27 minutes at a latitude of 40° North, 21 minutes at 50° North and only 11 minutes at 60° North. Contrast that with the full moon on March 27, 1975, when the delay was 75 minutes at 40° North, 84 minutes at 50° North and 97 minutes at 60° North.

If we multiply 29½ by 12, we get 354, the number of days in 12 lunar months, which is 11 less than 365 days. Thus the full moon in any calendar month usually occurs 11 days earlier in that month the next year. Of course, if the first full moon occurs on or before the 11th of the month, the one coming 354 days later will fall in the preceding month. In such a case, to find the date of the full moon in the same month one year later, add 19 days to the date. The same procedure applies to other lunar phases.

This is illustrated in the table giving the dates of new moon and full moon for January, April, July and October from 1977 through 1996. Only four months are given in the table, but the dates for the other months can be easily found by subtracting one day for each succeeding month. Because of the short month of February, the dates in April are usually only one or two days earlier than those in January.

Since the intervals from new moon to full moon and from full moon to new moon are both about 15 days, we can take half of that to get the dates of the half moon. By adding seven days to new moon to get first quarter and seven days to full moon to get last quarter, we can come within a day or two of the correct date.

The reason for listing the dates from 1977 to 1996 is to show that the lunar phases repeat themselves on the same calendar dates after 19 years, with a possible difference of one day, depending on the number of leap years involved. This period is called the Metonic cycle, being named after a Greek astronomer of the fifth century B.C. He found that 19 solar years are very nearly equal to 235 lunar months. Using modern values and multiplying the year of 365.2422 days by 19, we get 6939.6018 days. Multiplying the lunar month of 29.5306 days by 235, we get 6939.6910 days. The difference is only about two hours.

Dates of New Moon and Full Moon (1977–1996)

	January		*April*		*July*		*October*	
	New	Full	New	Full	New	Full	New	Full
1977	19	5	18	3	16	30	12	26
1978	8	24	7	22	5	19	2	16
1979	28	13	26	12	23	9	20	5
1980	17	2 & 31	14	30	12	27	9	23
1981	6	20	4	19	1 & 30	16	27	13
1982	24	9	23	8	20	6	16	2
1983	14	28	13	27	10	24	6	21
1984	3	17	1	15	28	12	24	9
1985	20	6	20	5	17	2	13	28
1986	10	25	9	24	6	21	3	17
1987	29	14	27	13	25	10	22	6
1988	19	3	16	2	13	28	10	24
1989	7	21	5	20	3	18	29	14
1990	26	10	24	9	21	7	18	4
1991	15	30	14	28	11	26	7	23
1992	4	19	3	16	29	14	25	11
1993	22	8	21	6	19	3	15	30
1994	11	27	10	25	8	22	4	19
1995	1	16	29	15	27	12	23	8
1996	20	5	17	3	15	30	12	26

13

The Moon's Path in the Sky

We are all familiar with the changes in the daily path of the sun across the sky during the year. Some of us may be puzzled by the speed with which the moon's path shifts its position. For example, in June in certain years the full moon rises almost in the southeast, the first and last quarter moons rise in the east, and the new moon rises almost in the northeast. In two weeks the moonrise point can shift about 70° along the horizon at Los Angeles and as much as 90° at Seattle. Also the highest altitude which the moon reaches each day varies considerably, having an extreme range of about 57° in two weeks.

The reason that the moon's position changes so much faster than the sun's is that the moon revolves around the earth in one month and the earth revolves around the sun in one year. On the average, the moon's monthly path in the sky is about the same as the sun's apparent annual path.

Since the earth's equator is tilted 23½° to its orbit, the sun appears to describe a circle called the ecliptic, which is inclined 23½° to the celestial equator. In Fig. 13-1, when the earth is at the summer position on June 21, the sun appears at the summer solstice, 23½° north of the equator.

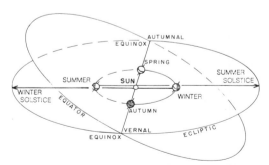

Fig. 13-1. As the earth moves around the sun during the year, the sun appears to move in the plane of the large circle marked "ecliptic." The circle marked "equator" is the projection of the earth's equator against the sky. The half of the ecliptic against which we see the sun during spring and summer is north of the equator and the other half is south of it.

From the earth's winter position on December 21 the sun appears at the winter solstice, 23½° south of the equator.

Since the sun's apparent position on the celestial sphere shifts from 23½° north of the equator to 23½° south of it, its noon altitude varies during the year by 47°. If the moon revolved around the earth in the same plane as that in which the earth revolves around the sun, the moon would follow the ecliptic and its meridian altitude would also vary by 47°. However, the moon's orbit is inclined about 5° to the earth's orbit. The moon can pass 5° north of the most northerly position of the sun and thus get 28½° north of the equator. Also it can pass 5° south of the most southerly position of the sun and thus get 28½° south of the equator. Therefore, the moon's meridian altitude can vary by 57°.

In Fig. 13-2 the circle passing through the north celestial pole and the zenith is the celestial meridian, which meets the horizon at the north and south points, marked N and S. The circle which meets the horizon at the east and west points (E and W) is the celestial equator, which is in the same plane as the earth's equator.

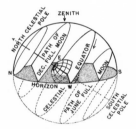

Fig. 13-2. The daily paths of the June and December full moons across the sky as seen from Los Angeles in 1987.

Suppose that the moon is full on December 21. Since the sun is then 23½° south of the equator at the winter solstice, the moon is near the summer solstice position, which is 23½° north of the equator. If it also happens to be 5° north of that point, its path in the sky is shown in Fig. 13.2 marked "Path of Dec. full moon." Contrast that with the circle marked "Path of June full moon."

We see how much the full moon, being opposite the sun, can change in six months. Now we wish to illustrate the changes in position of the moon at different phases during the four seasons of the year.

In each of the eight diagrams (Figs. 13-3–13-10) the sky is shown as seen from the latitude of Los Angeles. A few of the brighter stars and constellations are included. The heavy line marking the celestial equator always intersects the horizon at the east and west point. The dashed line marks the ecliptic, which is the apparent path of the sun during the year.

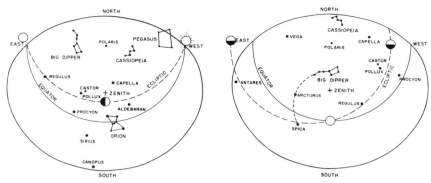

Fig. 13-3. (left) The sky at sunset in spring. The moon is shown at two different phases about one week apart. The first quarter moon is just south of the zenith and the full moon is at the eastern horizon. Fig. 13-4. (right) The sky at midnight in spring, when the first quarter moon is about to set. A week later the full moon is in the south, and after another week the last quarter moon is about to rise.

The sun is indicated by the circle with short lines radiating from it. The plain circle represents the full moon. The circle which is half black and half white represents the so-called half moon, which is the moon at first quarter or last quarter. The moon's position is marked on the ecliptic, but it may be as much as 5° from it.

Fig. 13-3 shows the sky at sunset in the spring, when the sun is at or near the vernal equinox and all of the northern half of the ecliptic is above the horizon. If the moon is at first quarter, it is at the position where the sun will be at the summer solstice on June 21. About a week later the moon is full and is at the position where the sun will be at the autumnal

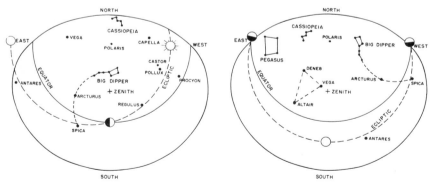

Fig. 13-5. (left) The sky near sunset in summer. The first quarter moon is not as high as it was in spring, and the full moon will rise some distance south of the east point. Fig. 13-6. (right)The sky at midnight in summer, when the full moon is near the sun's winter position and is very low in the south. The first quarter moon sets in the west and the last quarter moon rises in the east.

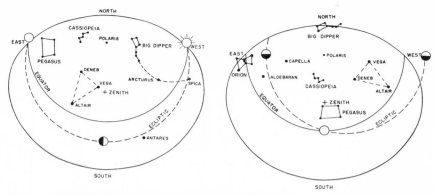

Fig. 13-7. (left) The autumn sky at sunset is the same as the summer sky at midnight (Fig. 13-6), but the moon's positions are shifted eastward by one phase. Fig. 13-8. (right) The autumn sky at midnight, with the full moon under the Square of Pegasus, and the last quarter moon north of Orion.

equinox on September 23. The full moon is opposite the sun and rises in the east at sunset.

Fig. 13-4 shows the sky six hours later, that is, at midnight in the spring. The first quarter moon is about to set a little north of the west point. The full moon is in the south. Since it is on the equator, it does not get as high as the first quarter moon, which is north of the equator. The last quarter moon comes about one week after full moon. It is south of the equator near the sun's position on December 21 (winter solstice). It rises a little south of the east point soon after midnight.

After three months the summer sky near sunset (Fig. 13-5) is the same

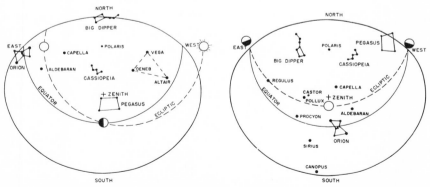

Fig. 13-9. (left) The winter sky just after sunset is the same as the autumn sky at midnight (Fig. 13-8), except for the shift of the moon's phases. Fig. 13-10. (right) The winter sky at midnight, when the full moon is near the zenith, being close to the sun's summer position.

as the spring sky at midnight (Fig. 13-4), except for the phases of the moon. The sun is at the summer solstice, the first quarter moon is at the autumnal equinox, and the full moon is at the winter solstice. Since the full moon is so far south, it does not get up very high. Its highest position is reached at midnight, which is shown in Fig. 13-6. Being opposite the sun, the summer full moon is near the sun's winter position. At Los Angeles on December 21 the noon sun is only 32½° high. It is possible for the summer full moon at midnight to be 5° lower, or only 27½° high.

Fig. 13-7 shows the autumn sky at sunset. Since the sun is on the equator, the full moon is also, and it follows the sun's path across the sky. The first quarter moon is low in the south, where the full moon was at midnight in summer. Fig. 13-7 is the same as Fig. 13-6, except that the moon's positions have been moved eastward by one quarter of a circle.

The full moon in autumn is near the vernal equinox just south of the Square of Pegasus. Its position at midnight is shown in Fig. 13-8. The same star map is used in Fig. 13-9 for the winter sky just after sunset. Now the first quarter moon is under the Square of Pegasus and the full moon is north of Orion.

In Fig. 13-10 the full moon at midnight is nearly overhead at the beginning of winter. It is where the sun is at the beginning of summer. Compare this with Fig. 13-6, where the summer full moon at midnight is much lower.

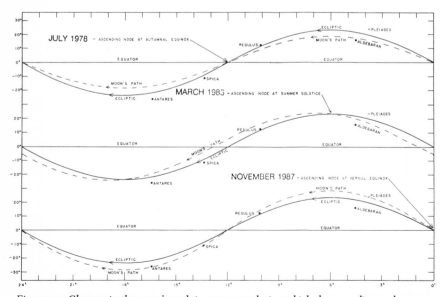

Fig. 13-11. Changes in the moon's path in 9.3 years, during which the ascending node moves westward from the autumnal equinox to the vernal equinox.

The moon's orbit is not fixed in position, because it is disturbed by the gravitational pull of the sun. Its points of intersection with the ecliptic, which are called nodes, are constantly shifting westward, making a complete circuit of the ecliptic in 18.6 years. This change is called the regression of the nodes and is similar to the westward motion of the equinoxes along the ecliptic called precession. That is very much slower, the period being nearly 26,000 years.

Fig. 13-11 shows how the moon's path changes during 9.3 years, half of the period of the regression of the nodes. The ascending node is the point where the moon's path crosses from the south side to the north side of the ecliptic. In July 1978 it will be at the autumnal equinox and the moon's path will be entirely inside the space bounded by the ecliptic and the equator. The right half of the moon's path lies south of the ecliptic, so that its maximum distance north of the equator is only 18½° (23½° − 5°). Similarly the most southerly point of the moon's path is 5° north of the ecliptic and only 18½° south of the equator.

The middle part of the diagram shows the moon's path in March 1983. In four years and eight months the nodes shift westward one quarter of the way around the ecliptic, so that the ascending node is at the summer solstice.

The lower part of the chart illustrates the situation in November 1987, when the ascending node is at the vernal equinox and the moon's path is entirely outside the space bounded by the ecliptic and the equator. Then the moon's path extends from 28½° north of the equator to 28½° south of it. Its range of 57° is 20° more than that in July 1978.

Lying close to the ecliptic are the Pleiades, Aldebaran, Regulus, Spica and Antares. As the moon's path shifts, it can pass in front of these objects at different times. Such a covering up of a star is called an occultation. Thus we can see how Aldebaran can be occulted by the moon for several years around the time shown in the upper part of the diagram. Then about nine years later the Pleiades, Regulus, Spica and Antares take their turns at being hidden by the moon, as shown in the lower part of the diagram. Since the moon moves its own diameter in about one hour, that is the maximum duration of each occultation.

The shifting positions of the moon are illustrated in the four pictures (Figs. 13-12–13-15) of the moon and the celestial circles in the planetarium sky of the Griffith Observatory. In each one the central vertical line is the southern half of the celestial meridian. The numbers along it indicate degrees of altitude measured from the south point of the horizon up to the zenith, which is marked 90°. The heavy line running from side to side is the celestial equator, with hours of right ascension marked along it.

The equator crosses the meridian at an altitude of 56°, which is 34° from the zenith. The zenith distance of the celestial equator is always equal to

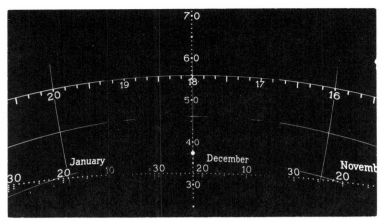

Fig. 13-12. The full moon near midnight in June 1978 will have a maximum altitude of 37½° at Los Angeles, as shown in the planetarium of the Griffith Observatory.

the latitude. Since Los Angeles is 34° north of the earth's equator, its zenith is 34° north of the celestial equator.

The dotted line going from side to side is the ecliptic, each dot marking the position of the sun on a particular date. Since the sun is 23½° north of the equator on June 22, its noon altitude on that date at Los Angeles is 79½° (56° + 23½°). Similarly its altitude on December 22 is 32½° (56° − 23½°), which is 47° lower.

The four pictures show the meridian altitude of the moon on four different dates when it is near the phase of full moon. The month appearing on the meridian differs by six months from the actual time, because the

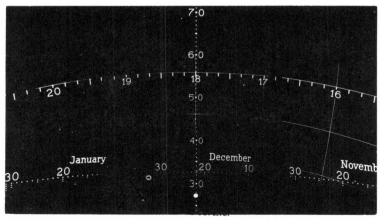

Fig. 13-13. The midnight full moon in June 1987 will have a maximum altitude of 27½° at Los Angeles. The vertical dotted line is the meridian. The horizontal dotted line is the ecliptic, the dates referring to the sun's position.

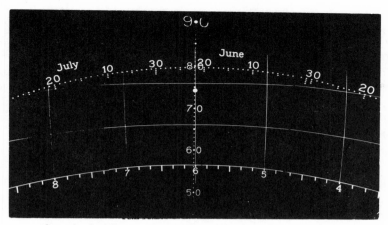

*Fig. 13-14. The midnight full moon in December 1978 will have a maximum altitude of 74½°
at Los Angeles. This is 5° less than the noon altitude of the sun on June 22.*

full moon is opposite the sun. For example, Fig. 13-12 shows December
on the meridian, but the actual month is June. The year is 1978, when
the moon's greatest declination is only 18½°. Its meridian altitude at
Los Angeles is 37½°. The data for the four pictures are as follows:

Fig.	Date	Declination	Altitude
13-12	June 1978	−18½°	37½°
13-13	June 1987	−28½°	27½°
13-14	Dec. 1978	+18½°	74½°
13-15	Dec. 1987	+28½°	84½°

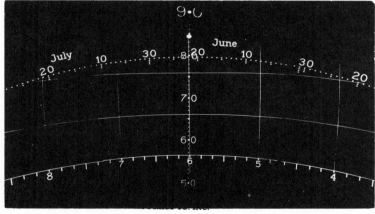

*Fig. 13-15. The midnight full moon in December 1987 will have a maximum altitude of 84½°
at Los Angeles. This is 5° more than the noon altitude of the sun on June 22.*

On the days when the moon reaches its highest altitude, it rises and sets farthest north, and remains above the horizon the longest time. For example, at a latitude of 42° North, the full moon in December 1987 will rise 40° north of the east point and set 40° north of the west point, remaining above the horizon for about 16 hours. On the other hand, the full moon in June 1987 will rise 40° south of the east point and set 40° south of the west point, remaining above the horizon for only 8 hours.

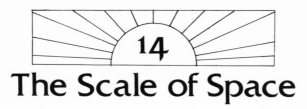

14

The Scale of Space

The distances of the stars are so much greater than any of the distances with which we are familiar that we find great difficulty in comprehending them. The coming of the space age with its trips to the moon and nearer planets has helped us to gain some idea of the size of the solar system, but no conception of how much farther away the stars are. It is hoped that this series of diagrams in which the scale is changed from one to the next will help the reader get a better understanding of the scale of space.

We start in Fig. 14-1 with the sizes of the earth and moon and the distance between them. In round numbers, the diameter of the earth is 8,000 miles and that of the moon is 2,000 miles. The distance between them is 240,000 miles, which is 30 times the earth's diameter or 60 times the earth's radius.

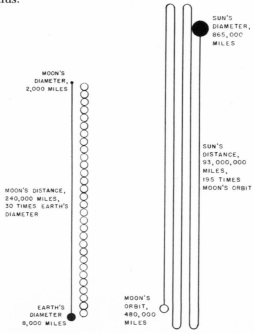

MOON'S DIAMETER, 2,000 MILES

MOON'S DISTANCE, 240,000 MILES, 30 TIMES EARTH'S DIAMETER

EARTH'S DIAMETER 8,000 MILES

MOON'S ORBIT, 480,000 MILES

SUN'S DIAMETER, 865,000 MILES

SUN'S DISTANCE, 93,000,000 MILES, 195 TIMES MOON'S ORBIT

Fig. 14-1 (left). Fig. 14-2 (right).

In Fig. 14-2 the earth-moon distance has been shrunk to $^1/_{60}$ its former size. The moon's orbit, having a diameter of 480,000 miles, is represented by the small circle at the lower left. The sun with a diameter of 865,000 miles is shown as a black disk at the upper right. The distance of 93,000,000 miles from the earth to the sun could not be shown as one straight line on this scale and so five parallel lines have been drawn. They have been connected so as to form a continuous line, which is 390 times as long as the radius of the circle representing the moon's orbit.

This kind of a line which goes up and down or back and forth is called a boustrophedon (pronounced with a long "e" and the accent on the third syllable). I first heard of this word in a course in navigation at the University of Michigan, where Dr. H. D. Curtis used it in describing his method of handing back papers to his students. It comes from the Greek, meaning "turning like oxen in plowing." It is also defined as an ancient mode of writing, in alternate directions, one line from left to right and the next from right to left (as fields are plowed). By turning Fig. 14-2 sideways, we can see why Dr. Curtis described it more briefly as a cow path up a hill.

Using the more accurate value of 2,160 miles for the moon's diameter, we find that the sun's diameter is 400 times greater. Since the sun's distance from the earth is also about 400 times greater than the moon's distance, the sun and the moon have about the same apparent size of half a degree. That is why a total eclipse of the sun is possible. Fig. 14-3 shows the moon's orbit drawn to scale on a photograph of the sun. The dot at the center representing the earth and the dot along the circle representing the moon should be slightly smaller to be exactly to scale.

Our next step is to change the scale by 390 times. As the small circle in Fig. 14-2 represents the moon's orbit around the earth, now the small circle in Fig. 14-4 represents the earth's orbit around the sun. Also shown are portions of the orbits of five other planets. Their distances from the sun in terms of the earth-sun distance (astronomical unit) are in round numbers: 5 for Jupiter, 10 for Saturn, 20 for Uranus, 30 for Neptune, and 40 for Pluto.

The long ellipse in Fig. 14-4 shows the size and shape of the orbit of Comet 1907 II Grigg-Mellish. This comet has the longest period of all the comets which have made more than one return to the sun during the time in which accurate records have been kept. The period of this comet is 164.3 years, almost exactly the same as the period of Neptune, which is 164.8 years. Therefore, its mean distance from the sun is about the same, namely, 30 astronomical units.

Since the eccentricity of this comet's orbit is 0.969, its distance from the sun varies from about one to 59 astronomical units. Thus the length of the ellipse, 60 astronomical units, is the same as the diameter of Neptune's orbit, which is very nearly a circle. Neptune is always about 30 astronomi-

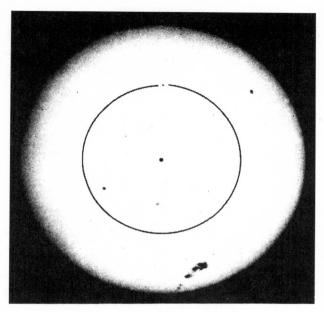

Fig. 14-3. Moon's orbit compared with sun.

cal units from the sun, but the comet can get nearly twice as far away. There are many comets which travel very much farther out in space, but they have been seen in each case at only one approach to the sun. Their periods are not known, but they must run into thousands of years. Also their maximum distances from the sun must be expressed in hundreds of astronomical units.

The comets are the most distant members of our solar system. Beyond them lie the stars. The nearest star is at a distance of 272,000 astronomical units. This is about 4,500 times the size of the orbit of Comet 1907 II. Fig. 14-5 helps one to visualize that ratio. The tiny ellipse about one-sixteenth of an inch long at the lower left represents the comet's orbit. The dot (not to scale) at the lower right represents the nearest star, Alpha Centauri. The line connecting them is about 23 feet long and represents the distance between them, about 25 trillion (25,000,000,000,000) miles.

It may help one to comprehend this distance if we emphasize the analogy of plowing a field. If our plow travels with the speed of light, it makes a furrow from the sun to the earth in eight minutes and plows through the last of the comet's dust at the end of a working day of eight hours. It reaches the end of our field pictured in Fig. 14-5 after about 80 such eight-hour days. Then it turns around and spends another 80 days making the next furrow. This process is continued for about 13 years, until we fi-

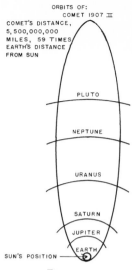

ORBITS OF:
COMET 1907 Ⅱ

COMET'S DISTANCE,
5,500,000,000
MILES, 59 TIMES
EARTH'S DISTANCE
FROM SUN

PLUTO

NEPTUNE

URANUS

SATURN

JUPITER

EARTH

SUN'S POSITION

Fig. 14-4.

nally plow into the nearest star. If we had worked 24 hours a day, as light does, we would have reached the star in 4.3 years.

Distances of stars are commonly expressed in light-years. One light-year is the distance travelled by light in one year. It is equal to nearly six trillion miles. The nearest star is 4.3 light-years away.

To appreciate the length of a light-year, let us notice the following relations. A light-year is 63,310 astronomical units. In one mile there are 63,360 inches. Therefore, on a map on which the earth is one inch from the sun, a light-year would be represented almost exactly by one mile. The nearest star would appear on such a map 4.3 miles from the sun, whereas Pluto, the farthest planet, would be only 40 inches away. This is a convenient scale to remember: if one inch equals one astronomical unit, then one mile equals one light-year.

The number of stars within a given distance of the sun is uncertain, because there may be some very faint stars in our neighborhood whose distances have not yet been found. However, for our purposes here we are not so much concerned with the number of stars as with the distances to which they extend. We may not be far off if we use the round numbers of 10 stars in a sphere with a radius of 10 light-years. Also we shall assume the same density of stars in the space throughout our galaxy.

The diagrams in Fig. 14-6 illustrate the size of our galaxy. The first circle (A) represents a cross section of a sphere with a radius of 10 light-years and with the sun at the center. Within this sphere we are assuming that there are 10 stars, though the actual number known today is a few more than that, if we count the separate components of double star systems.

The second large circle (B) represents a cross section of a sphere with a radius of 100 light-years, and so circle A is $^1/_{10}$ its former size. Since the volume of a sphere varies as the cube of the radius, the second sphere has a volume 1000 times that of the first and should contain about 10,000 stars. In a similar manner, circle C represents a cross section of a sphere with a radius of 1000 light-years containing 10,000,000 stars.

The radius of circle D is only 5 times that of circle C, so that the volume increases in this case by only 125 times, making the number of stars in this sphere 1,250,000,000. Finally, we reach the limits of our galaxy, which is shaped like a cartwheel, with a diameter of about 100,000 light-years and a thickness of about 10,000 light-years. In the diagram it is shown edgewise, surrounded by tiny circles representing globular clusters. There are about 100 of these clusters, each of which contains more than 100,000 stars.

It is not possible to observe all the stars in our galaxy. In addition to the great distances which make most stars too faint to be detected, there are clouds of dust and gas (like the smog of our cities) which dim the farthest stars a great deal. However, the globular clusters can be observed to great distances and they form a symmetrical system around our galaxy.

Using a diameter of 100,000 light-years, which is ten times the diameter of our last sphere in the diagram, we can assume a volume which is

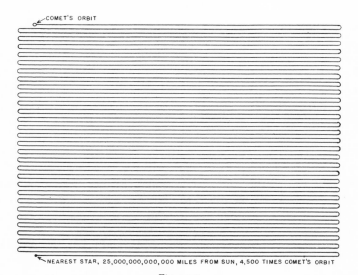

COMET'S ORBIT

NEAREST STAR, 25,000,000,000,000 MILES FROM SUN, 4,500 TIMES COMET'S ORBIT

Fig. 14-5.

100 times as great. This gives us a figure of 125 billion (125,000,000,000) stars in our galaxy. This result is very uncertain, but is consistent with estimates made from other data.

The Milky Way is our edge-on, inside view of our galaxy. The light of the Milky Way is produced by the combined light of many very faint, closely crowded stars which can not be resolved by the naked eye. In the comparatively open sky on either side of the Milky Way we can observe other galaxies. The nearest of these are the two Magellanic Clouds, which might be called satellites of our galaxy, because of their nearness and smaller size.

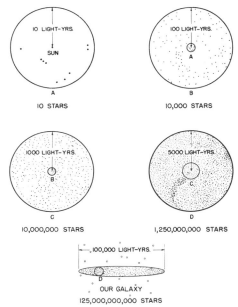

Fig. 14-6. Our sun among the stars. The circles represent cross sections of spheres centered at the sun. Our galaxy is shown edgewise, surrounded by globular clusters.

A similar triple system consists of the great spiral galaxy in Andromeda and its two small companions. This group is at a distance of over two million light-years. The Andromeda Galaxy is somewhat larger than our own galaxy and can be seen with the unaided eye in a dark sky. This is a good place for us to stop in exploring this small sample of space, because we have reached the limit of naked-eye visibility.

Summarizing, we can return to the earth and see how long it would take a spacecraft to travel to the nearest star. We shall use round numbers and a modest speed of ten thousand miles an hour. Since the moon is 240,000 miles away, we would reach it in 24 hours. Since the sun is nearly

400 times farther than the moon, we would pass it after a little over one year. We would cross the orbit of the last planet, Pluto, after 40 years. However, we would not live long enough to reach the nearest star. Our descendants might make it, but they would be our descendants ten thousand generations later. Only one day to the moon, but ten thousand generations at ten thousand miles an hour to the nearest star. Probably long before they reached there, they would forget why they started out on their journey.

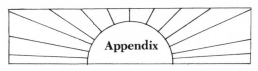

Appendix

A Constellation Quiz

In making a star map, we usually connect the brightest stars in a constellation with straight lines to make a simple figure like a triangle, a square, a cross, or a dipper. Most people know the Big Dipper, which is a part of Ursa Major, the Big Bear, but very few can find the stars which are supposed to outline the animal. Similarly, we recognize Cassiopeia as a W, Pegasus as a square, and Cygnus as a cross.

The outlines of forty constellations are shown in two accompanying pages. There is no system in their arrangement, except that the smaller ones are at the beginning and the larger ones at the end. Mapmakers differ sometimes as to how the lines connecting the stars should be drawn, but there is general agreement on most of the constellations.

The size of a dot indicates the brightness of a star. Occasionally a star of the fourth or fifth magnitude has been included to complete the outline of the figure, but otherwise the stars are limited to third magnitude or brighter. Sometimes a fairly bright star may be omitted if it does not seem to add anything helpful to the figure.

It is suggested that the reader first look at the outlines of those forty numbered constellations and see how many can be identified. Then the following numbered descriptions can be read. They contain hints which should help in recognizing some more of them. Finally, the maps can be referred to. The answers to the quiz will be found at the end of the chapter. Here we go with the helpful hints.

1. We start with one of the hardest, which contains only two stars brighter than the fourth magnitude. The brightest star in the constellation is a visual double star. The faint companion was found a half century after its existence had been predicted in 1844 by Friedrich Wilhelm Bessel from the variable motion of the primary star. Bessel also predicted the existence of the companion of Sirius. Both these companions are white dwarf stars, which have very high densities. This constellation No. 1 rises at about the same time as Sirius.

2. This little triangle marks the head of an animal belonging to the zodiac. About 2,000 years ago the vernal equinox was in this constellation, but precession (a very slow, wobbling motion of the earth) has shifted this point into the next constellation to the west.

3. Another triangle appears just north of No. 2. Like Andromeda, which is just west of it, it contains a spiral galaxy (M33) belonging to the local group of galaxies.

4. The two northern stars of this group, which looks like the spanker sail of a ship, point toward Spica. Hence it has been known to the sailors as "Spica's Spanker." The real name is that of a bird.

5. A missile which is located just south of Cygnus.

6. A marine mammal attaining a length of from six to eight feet.

7. A musical instrument containing the fifth brightest star, which will become the pole star in about 12,000 years as a result of the earth's precessional motion. The northeast star of this triangle can be seen as a double star and the telescope reveals it as made of four stars. The southwest star of the parallelogram is a famous eclipsing binary and just east of it is the best known of the planetary nebulae.

8. The shape of this constellation suggests its name. It contains a star lettered "R" after which a class of variable stars is named. This star is of the sixth magnitude most of the time. At irregular intervals it decreases in brightness, occasionally becoming as faint as the fourteenth magnitude. The decrease is very rapid, usually taking only a few days, but the recovery is slower, sometimes lasting many months.

The star T in this constellation is one of the few known cases of a repeating nova. In 1946 it increased in brightness about 1,500 times from the eleventh magnitude to the third. It immediately began to fade and disappear from naked-eye view. A similar explosion occurred in 1866.

9. South of Orion is this fast-moving animal, which is apparently being chased by the Big Dog.

10. This "W" stands for a vain and conceited woman, who was punished by being forced to spend half of her time upside down as she swings under the North Star. Tycho's supernova appeared in this area in 1572, rivalling Venus in brightness and being visible in the daytime for several weeks. It was observed with the unaided eye for about 16 months.

Gamma, the middle star of the "W," is normally of the second magnitude, but in 1936 it began to grow brighter and later it became fainter than normal. Its range of magnitude was from 1.6 to 3.0.

11. Southwest of Fomalhaut and visible along the southern horizon for only a few months on autumn evenings, this inconspicuous constellation bears the name of a wading bird, having a long, straight bill and long legs and neck.

12. The four eastern stars of this figure form the bowl of what is called the "Milk Dipper," since it lies in the Milky Way. The four western stars form a weapon and a missile (the same as No. 5), which is being aimed by this creature at the Scorpion. The eight stars together form a teapot. This constellation of the zodiac contains the winter solstice, the point occupied by the sun on December 21. Also the center of the galaxy is located in this region of the sky.

13. This is the only constellation in the zodiac which is not an animal. It was once a part of the Scorpion, forming its claws. This is shown by the names of the two stars at the upper right of this figure. Parents who want to name their children after stars might use these for twins: Zubenelgenubi (southern claw) and Zubeneschamali (northern claw).

About 2,000 years ago the sun was in this constellation at the time of the autumnal equinox. The equality of day and night furnishes a clue to its name.

14. The earth's axis points almost directly toward the star at the end of the tail of this animal, which has been swinging around the north celestial pole for

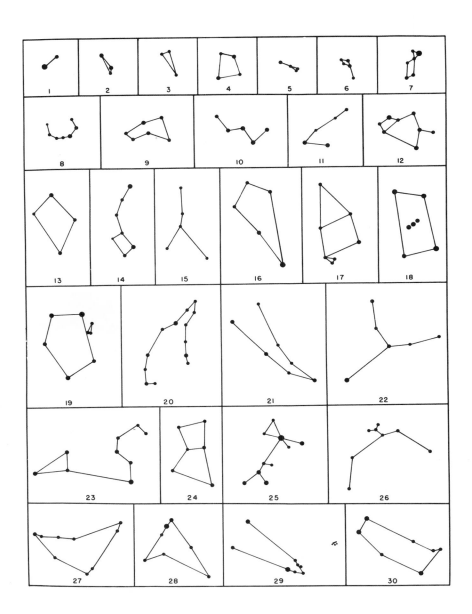

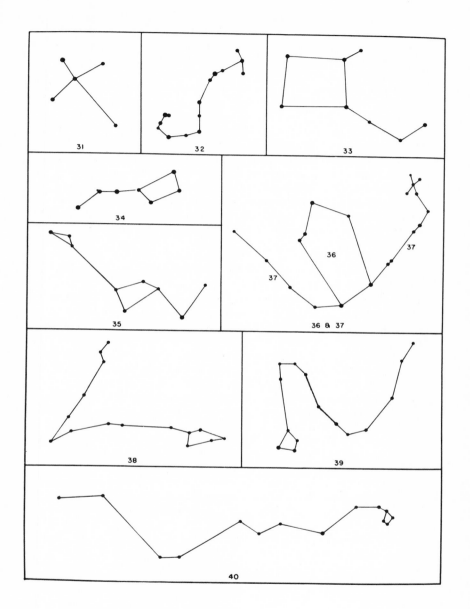

so many years that it has been very much stretched. The shape of the figure suggests the other name of this group.

15. A very faint constellation of the zodiac, having no stars brighter than the fourth magnitude. Its name is part of the name of one of the circles on the earth, because the sun was in this constellation at the time of the summer solstice about 2,000 years ago. It is also the name of a disease. The feature of this region is a cluster of stars known as Praesepe and more commonly called the "Bee Hive."

16. We see here the outline of a kite or an ice cream cone. At the bottom of the cone is the star which was used to open the World's Fair in Chicago in 1933. It is the fastest of all the bright stars, moving across the sky at about 70 miles a second. Even at this high speed it will take about 800 years to move half a degree, the angular diameter of the moon.

17. The King of Ethiopia includes a variable star designated Delta followed by the genitive case of his name. This star gives the name to the class of variable stars by whose special characteristics we can measure the distances of globular clusters and galaxies.

18. The finest constellation in the whole sky contains seven stars which are among the 67 brightest. The star at the upper left corner is red because of its relatively low temperature. It was the first star whose angular diameter was measured with the interferometer. Because of uncertainty in its distance, its linear diameter is not accurately known, but it is certainly larger than the diameter of the earth's orbit around the sun. The star at the lower right corner is blue, because it is very much hotter.

A long-exposure photograph of this constellation shows it enveloped in nebulosity, the brightest part of which can be seen with the naked eye under the best conditions.

19. This is commonly represented as a pentagon, but the lower left star marking one foot of this man really belongs to Taurus. The star at the upper right corner is the sixth brightest star in the entire sky and the fourth brightest of all stars seen in northerly latitudes. It marks a goat and below it is a small triangle marking two little kids. At the apex of the triangle is Epsilon, an eclipsing binary with a period of twenty-seven years, the longest known.

20. The feature of this group is the "Demon Star," which winks at us once in 2 days and 21 hours, because of the eclipse of one star by its faint companion. Located in this area is the radiant of a meteor shower which is seen every August.

21. This lady was saved by No. 20. Located in this direction is a galaxy which is visible to the unaided eye under good conditions.

22. The brightest star in this Y-shaped figure marks a spike or an ear of wheat or corn, which is being held by this goddess. She seems to be a symbol of the harvest, since the sun appears in front of her in September.

23. The head of this animal is marked by a sickle or a reversed question mark. The hind-quarters are defined by a triangle, the left star of which is at the tip of his tail. A famous shower of meteors radiates from the sickle in November.

24. When this celebrated hero in mythology was placed in the sky, it looks as

if a trick was played on him. He looks more like a butterfly than anything else. A globular cluster in this region is one of the showpieces of the sky.

25. In the head of this animal is the brightest appearing of all the stars.

26. This man is a symbol of the rainy season, since the rains occurred at the time when the sun was in the direction of this constellation.

27. It has given us the name of one of the circles on the earth, because the sun was in this region at the time of the winter solstice about 2,000 years ago.

28. The figure of this king of birds is commonly used as an emblem of heraldry. The brightest star in it forms with Vega and Deneb what is known as the "Summer Triangle."

29. The head of this animal is marked by a group of stars in the shape of a V. At the upper left is Aldebaran, marking one eye. The other stars in the V belong to a star cluster called the Hyades. To the northwest we find the Pleiades, a famous star cluster which is also called the Seven Sisters.

30. Northeast of Orion are two bright stars about 4° apart and of nearly the same brilliance. There is no other pair of stars of equal brightness so close together in the northern half of the sky. Hence this constellation is well named.

31. The shape of this figure suggests its popular name. Its official name is that of a large aquatic bird. The tail is marked by a bright star, whose name means "tail" in Arabic. Near it is the North America Nebula.

32. This is the finest constellation of the zodiac and it really looks like its name. The brightest star in it is a giant, red star, whose name means the "rival of Mars."

33. By including one star in Andromeda, we can draw this "Great Square," which marks the body of the animal. It has been given wings and is flying upside down, the neck and head being marked by the three stars from the lower right corner.

34. The most familiar group of stars is part of an animal whose tail was stretched as she was carried by it from the earth to the sky. The pair of stars at the right end are the pointers to the North Star. The middle star of the three at the left is Mizar, the first double star to be discovered. Each of its components is also double, as is Alcor, the fainter star which can be seen with the unaided eye very close to Mizar.

35. The most famous star here is Mira, the first known variable star. It lies nearly half way between the triangle and the quadrilateral, but it is not shown, because it is invisible to the naked eye most of the time.

36 and 37. These two are considered together, because the first one is holding the second. He holds the middle of the creature, with the tail to the east and the head to the west marked by an X. These rather faint constellations are in the summer sky.

38. The vernal equinox is now located in this very faint constellation. A clear, moonless sky away from city lights is needed to see it. The widespread V of stars represents ribbons tied to the tails of two animals which live at almost all latitudes of the earth.

39. This fabulous animal winds around between the Big Bear and the Little Bear. It contains Thuban, the pole star at the time when the pyramids were being built in Egypt.

40. This is the longest and largest constellation, having a length of 108° and an average width of 12°. Its area of 1,303 square degrees is 19 times the area of the Southern Cross, the smallest constellation. Its head, marked by four stars, is a little east of Procyon and the end of its tail is a little west of Antares. Its full extent of nearly one-third of a circle is not shown in the diagram. It is a faint constellation, having no stars of the first magnitude and only one of the second.

This completes our list of forty constellations. Altogether there are eighty-eight, but many of them are too faint to be included here and others are too far south to be observed from our latitudes.

The names and meanings of our forty constellations are as follows:

Name	*Meaning*
1. Canis Minor	Little Dog
2. Aries	Ram
3. Triangulum	Triangle
4. Corvus	Crow
5. Sagitta	Arrow
6. Delphinus	Dolphin
7. Lyra	Lyre
8. Corona Borealis	Northern Crown
9. Lepus	Hare
10. Cassiopeia	Cassiopeia
11. Grus	Crane
12. Sagittarius	Archer
13. Libra	Balance
14. Ursa Minor	Little Bear
15. Cancer	Crab
16. Bootes	Bear Driver
17. Cepheus	Cepheus
18. Orion	Orion
19. Auriga	Charioteer
20. Perseus	Perseus
21. Andromeda	Andromeda
22. Virgo	Virgin
23. Leo	Lion
24. Hercules	Hercules
25. Canis Major	Big Dog
26. Aquarius	Water Carrier
27. Capricornus	Sea Goat
28. Aquila	Eagle
29. Taurus	Bull
30. Gemini	Twins
31. Cygnus	Swan

32.	Scorpius	Scorpion
33.	Pegasus	Winged Horse
34.	Ursa Major	Big Bear
35.	Cetus	Whale
36.	Ophiuchus	Serpent Holder
37.	Serpens	Serpent
38.	Pisces	Fishes
39.	Draco	Dragon
40.	Hydra	Water Monster

INDEX